# Hakeem Olajuwon: The Remarkable Story of One of 90s Basketball's Greatest Centers

An Unauthorized Biography

By: Clayton Geoffreys

Copyright © 2016 by Calvintir Books, LLC

All rights reserved. Neither this book nor any portion thereof may be reproduced or used in any manner whatsoever without the express written permission. Published in the United States of America.

**Disclaimer**: The following book is for entertainment and informational purposes only. The information presented is without contract or any type of guarantee assurance. While every caution has been taken to provide accurate and current information, it is solely the reader's responsibility to check all information contained in this article before relying upon it. Neither the author nor publisher can be held accountable for any errors or omissions.

Under no circumstances will any legal responsibility or blame be held against the author or publisher for any reparation, damages, or monetary loss due to the information presented, either directly or indirectly. This book is not intended as legal or medical advice. If any such specialized advice is needed, seek a qualified individual for help.

Trademarks are used without permission. Use of the trademark is not authorized by, associated with, or sponsored by the trademark owners. All trademarks and brands used within this book are used with no intent to infringe on the trademark owners and only used for clarifying purposes.

This book is not sponsored by or affiliated with the National Basketball Association, its teams, the players, or anyone involved with them.

Visit my website at www.claytongeoffreys.com

Cover photo by University of Houston Digital Library is licensed under CC BY 2.0 / modified from original

# Table of Contents

Foreword ................................................................................. 1

Introduction ............................................................................ 3

Chapter 1: Childhood and Early Life ................................... 7

Chapter 2: High School Years ............................................... 9

Chapter 3: College Years at the University of Houston ...... 11

    Freshman Year .................................................................. 11

    Sophomore Year ............................................................... 11

    Junior Year ........................................................................ 15

Chapter 4: Hakeem's NBA Career ....................................... 17

    Getting Drafted ................................................................. 17

    Rookie Season .................................................................. 20

    First Finals Appearance .................................................... 23

    Fall From the Top ............................................................. 29

    Becoming the Lone Tower, Several First-Round Exits ..... 33

    Missing the Playoffs ......................................................... 45

Improved Offensive Repertoire, Defensive Player of the Year, Return to the Postseason ....................................................... 47

First Season MVP, Second DPOY, First NBA Title, First Finals MVP ........................................................................... 52

Second NBA Championship ................................................ 61

Failure to Three-Peat ............................................................ 70

Reinforced by Barkley, the Houston Big Three .................... 73

Injury Season, First-Round Exits ......................................... 78

More Injuries, Missing the Playoffs ..................................... 83

Final Season in Houston ....................................................... 85

Trade to the Raptors, Final NBA Season, Retirement .......... 86

Chapter 5: Olajuwon's Personal Life .................................... 91

Chapter 6: Impact on Basketball ........................................... 95

Chapter 7: Olajuwon's Legacy and Future .......................... 103

Final Word/About the Author ............................................. 106

# Foreword

Hakeem Olajuwon has cemented a legacy as one of the greatest big men to ever play the game of basketball. Known for his 'Dream Shake' signature move, he inspired the next generation of big men like Tim Duncan and Dwight Howard by demonstrating the versatility a big man could have on the basketball court. To this day, he remains a beloved centerpiece of the Houston Rockets organization and remembered as a class act champion. The 1990s were a different time in basketball, when superstars would stay with teams for decades, as seen with legends like Karl Malone and Michael Jordan. Hakeem was no exception, igniting the city of Houston every night in the Toyota Center. Thank you for purchasing *Hakeem Olajuwon: The Remarkable Story of One of 90s Basketball's Greatest Centers*. In this unauthorized biography, we will learn Hakeem Olajuwon's incredible life story and impact on the game of basketball. Hope you enjoy and if you do, please do not forget to leave a review!

Also, check out my website at claytongeoffreys.com to join my exclusive list where I let you know about my latest books. To thank you for your purchase, you can go to my site to download a free copy of *33 Life Lessons: Success Principles, Career Advice & Habits of Successful People*. In the book, you'll learn from some of the greatest thought leaders of different industries on what it takes to become successful and how to live a great life.

Cheers,

*Clayton Geoffreys*

*Visit me at www.claytongeoffreys.com*

# Introduction

The NBA is typically a dream for most young boys who pick up a basketball. Those that do defy the odds and play professionally usually start playing the game early as kids and continue to play on a slew of school and club teams throughout their childhood and youth. Most, if not, all of those kids grew up watching their sports idols winning championships and MVPs while making millions of dollars. They grew up emulating and idolizing those players in the hope of following a similar career path in the future. Those kids start at a young age—where imagination and dreams are larger than life.

Not many professional athletes begin to play their chosen sport at age 15 – basketball or otherwise. Not many have a name that translates to "always being on top." Not many handball players get asked to join the high school basketball team, not too many players defy odds to travel all the way from Nigeria to the United States and years later get enshrined into the Naismith Memorial Basketball Hall of Fame in Springfield, Mass.

It has definitely been a dream ride for Hakeem "The Dream" Olajuwon, who went from knowing very little about the game of basketball as a youth to becoming an integral part of one of college basketball's more memorable squads and one of the NBA's all-time greatest players.

Hakeem Olajuwon, regarded as one of the greatest centers in the history of the NBA, is a proven winner on every stage he's played basketball on. In the NBA, he was a two-time champion, a two-time finals MVP, a regular-season MVP, a 12-time All-Star, a 12-time All-NBA Team member, a two-time Defensive Player of the Year, and a nine-time All-Defensive Team member. However, merely looking at his accomplishments as a player does not totally describe or explain The Dream's career.

If you look at the history of the NBA, there have been more than a dozen great centers to grace the league's hardwood floors. You talk about a guy like Bill Russell, who made his name by winning championships with his defense and rebounding. Then there's Wilt Chamberlain, the man who ruled under the basket and scored 100 points in a single game. Years later, Kareem Abdul-Jabbar piled up over 38,000 career points by scoring over defenders with his patented skyhook. Then Shaquille O'Neal dominated every other center he faced using his size, strength, and skill. Every great center in the NBA was known for one or two things on either offense or defense. Hakeem Olajuwon was different.

Olajuwon dominated on both ends of the floor like nobody else the NBA has ever had. On offense, he was perhaps the most skilled center in NBA history. His footwork and grace on the floor made guards look like garbage. His quick feet and ball handles continually threw opposing centers off balance. And Hakeem's bevy of pump fakes and pivot moves made it seem as if he was dancing without the music. No other center in history has ever displayed those offensive skills. On defense, Olajuwon was no slacker. His quick feet allowed him to rotate quickly to the open spot on the floor. With his length and athleticism, together with his natural skills of anticipation, Hakeem could get up to the rim to swat away shots with ease. That's why he holds the NBA record for career blocks. While those are usual skills that defensive centers have, what put Olajuwon on a different pedestal is that fact that he got more steals than even most guards. He honed that defensive ability using his quick feet and fast hands to get easy deflections on passing lanes. It's no wonder why his name was always a staple on NBA All-Defensive teams.

What made Hakeem Olajuwon even better was that he accomplished everything in his NBA career at the time of the golden age of the center position. As good as Bill Russell was, his best rival was merely Wilt Chamberlain. Kareem, though his career spanned two decades, initially played in an era when the NBA was at its weakest. On the other hand, Olajuwon played and was immensely successful against the likes of Moses Malone, Patrick Ewing, Bill Laimbeer, Robert Parish, David Robinson, Alonzo Mourning, and Shaquille O'Neal. Those are some of the toughest centers in history. Despite playing against those household names, Hakeem was head and shoulders the best of the crop. That's what makes him one of the greatest centers in NBA history, and possibly even the absolute best.

# Chapter 1: Childhood and Early Life

Born in Lagos, Nigeria on Jan. 21, 1963, Hakeem Abdul Olajuwon was the third of six children of Salaam and Abike Olajuwon, who owned a cement business in Lagos– Nigeria's most populous city. Hakeem and his siblings were raised in a one-story, three-bedroom red concrete house in a small, middle-class neighborhood in Lagos. It was there that Olajuwon was taught by his parents to always be honest, to work hard, to respect his elders, and to believe in himself.

Olajuwon was a two-sport athlete in soccer and handball at his high school – Muslim Teachers College – when a fellow student asked the then 6-foot-9 inch, 170-pound Olajuwon to join the basketball team. Soccer dominates the sporting scene in Nigeria so, not surprisingly; Olajuwon had originally taken his natural physical abilities and his athletic frame to the soccer pitch as well as the handball court. His experience as a soccer player is one of the reasons that his footwork is beyond comparison for a big man.

Though he was new to basketball, Olajuwon was a natural fit for the game. He grasped the sport right away, fascinated by the ball-handling skills and dribbling techniques that he saw from his classmates. Olajuwon was able to take advantage of his size and agility and the tremendous hand-to-eye coordination and footwork he had honed from years of playing handball and as a soccer goalkeeper. Hard work was needed to overcome the fact that basketball was not televised in Nigeria – which made it difficult for Olajuwon to see how basketball's best played the game.

Perhaps his quick adaptation to the sport of basketball stemmed in part from the simple advice that he received from those who steered the handball player toward basketball: "Stay in the middle and block every shot that comes in your direction" (advice that would soon see him averaging more than five blocks per game in college). Two years later, he found himself playing major college basketball in the United States at the University of Houston, turning his team into a regular contender on the game's brightest stage.

## Chapter 2: High School Years

Olajuwon was not highly scouted by American colleges as a high school student in Nigeria, even though as a 17-year-old he had led the Nigerian national basketball team to a third-place finish in the All-African tournament in 1979. His relatively short high school basketball career first drew attention at the international tournament in Angola. An opposing coach at the tournament was so impressed by Olajuwon's blossoming game that he encouraged Olajuwon to consider playing college basketball in the United States. That same coach passed along Olajuwon's name to then University of Houston head coach Guy Lewis. Luckily for the Cougars, Olajuwon began his first trip to America in New York, which was a bit cold and blustery for the native Nigerian. Upon arriving in Houston, however, he could not help but notice the beautiful oak trees and great architecture. The hot and humid southeastern Texas bayou weather reminded Olajuwon of his home in Nigeria, allowing the future star to feel right at home. The recruitment of Olajuwon came during a time in college basketball when coaches did not place much emphasis on scouting international players and having them come to college in the United States. However, the Cougars felt they had someone special in Olajuwon and convinced the young Nigerian that Houston was the place for him. Olajuwon enrolled at Houston under the name Akeem Abdul Olajuwon – a name he would use throughout college and into his early NBA days, until officially adopting the spelling "Hakeem" in March of 1991.

Though he grew up in a middle-class family in Nigeria, Olajuwon still did not play with the proper footwear until he began college at the University of Houston. It was when he was a Cougar by the time Olajuwon and his size 16 feet were finally able to play basketball without pain and with proper basketball shoes on his feet.

# Chapter 3: College Years at the University of Houston

## Freshman Year

Olajuwon redshirted his first season at Houston and then played only limited minutes in his first playing season, averaging just 18.2 minutes of playing time, with 8.3 points, 6.2 rebounds and 2.5 blocks per game) in 1981-82. The team had overall success that season, advancing to the first of three consecutive NCAA Final Four appearances. The Houston Cougars fell to James Worthy, Michael Jordan, and the North Carolina Tar Heels in the NCAA semifinals that year. Afterward, Olajuwon asked his coaches how he could improve as a player and the answer was practice sessions with future NBA Hall of Famer Moses Malone, who was playing for the Houston Rockets at the time.

## Sophomore Year

The sessions with Malone must have worked for Olajuwon, who also added bulk to his previously slender frame by eating plenty of steak and ice cream. Now standing at an even 7 feet tall, he increased his averages during the 1982-83 season to 13.9 points, 11.4 rebounds, and 5.1 blocks a game, and he morphed from a curiosity to an acknowledged talent in college basketball. As a sophomore, Olajuwon, Drexler, and the rest of the Cougars were perhaps college basketball's most dominant team, posting a 31-3 overall regular-season record en route to the school's first-ever Southwest Conference regular-season title with a perfect 16-0 conference record.

On the heels of the team's 1982 NCAA Final Four appearance and Houston's strong start to their 1982-83 season, Olajuwon and his teammates began to receive national notoriety for their style of play. Houston's high-flying offense featured a playground-inspired brand of basketball that celebrated the dunk. It stood in polar opposite to the fundamentally strong, methodical, and structured style of play that UCLA and head coach John Wooden popularized during the Bruins' run of 10 NCAA National Championships in 11 seasons from 1964-75. Wooden's players were even banned from dunking the ball for much of Wooden's tenure at the school, so the Houston

Cougars of the early-to-mid 1980's stood in strong contrast to the established coaching teachings of the day.

To Houston head coach Guy Lewis, dunking was a vital part of his team's offense and considered a preferred play to the jump shot – not an unnecessary showboating move as viewed by traditional coaches at the time. Lewis encouraged his players to play loose and quickly as he emphasized athleticism over fundamentalism in his game planning. Olajuwon's teammates, who had grown up in the U.S., had been influenced by the excitement of playground basketball in the 1970's and the way that the ABA was changing the game with its high-flying talents, such as future Hall of Famer Julius Erving, and the upstart professional league's All-Star Game and dunk contest. While the Nigerian-born Olajuwon did not grow up playing basketball in this style – or any style for that matter – his natural athletic ability fit right in with Lewis' coaching. The quick footwork and reflexes he gained from years of handball and soccer as a youth made him a natural pledge for what would be known as the unofficial fraternity of "Phi Slama Jama."

Since the team played such a different brand of basketball, it was only fitting that they would earn a nickname that captured the Cougars' preference for fast breaks over set plays. Houston Post sportswriter Thomas Bonk coined the phrase "Phi Slama Jama" in a January 1983 article to describe Texas' tallest fraternity. The Phi Slama Jama moniker became so ingrained in the program's culture that the nickname was included on the team's warm-up suits as the season went on. It was also a fraternity that featured individual nicknames that captured their unique talents. Hakeem was named "The Dream" and Clyde was called "The Glide." The others bore similar nicknames that described how they played on the court.

Houston once again advanced to the Final Four in 1983, defeating an equally athletic and offensive-minded Louisville team (featuring their own nickname, "The Doctors of Dunk") before falling to underdog North Carolina State 54-52 on a buzzer-beating shot. That game was the closest that Olajuwon came to winning an NCAA Championship despite advancing to the Final Four in all three of his eligible seasons. The game against North

Carolina State became one of college basketball's most talked-about upset victories, thanks in part to the personality of the late Wolf Pack head coach Jim Valvano and the perceived dominance of Phi Slama Jama. Despite the loss, Olajuwon was named the tournament's Most Outstanding Player; he is the last player to receive that honor as a member of the team that lost the championship game.

## Junior Year

Olajuwon again took his game to new heights in what turned out to be his final season at the University of Houston. In addition to averaging his collegiate high of 16.8 PPG, he also led the nation with 13.5 rebounds per game, 5.6 blocks per game, and a .675 field goal percentage. Olajuwon earned consensus First Team All-American honors as he led his team to a 32-5 record. The Cougars made a repeat trip to the NCAA Championship Game, but fell short once again, this time losing to future NBA All-Star Patrick Ewing and the Georgetown Hoyas. The battle between Ewing and Olajuwon was just the start of a long parallel career path between the two future

Basketball Hall-of-Famers that also featured an NBA finals matchup.

Olajuwon's collegiate career years later earned him the honor of being named the Southwest Conference Player of the Decade for the 1980's. He also had his number retired at the University of Houston, along with Drexler's. With the end of Olajuwon's collegiate career and the departure of integral teammate Michael Young following the 1984 Championship game Final after the previous season's departures of Drexler and teammate Larry Micheaux, Phi Slama Jama was officially grounded.

# Chapter 4: Hakeem's NBA Career

## Getting Drafted

Olajuwon may have begun his college career as an unheralded player, but coming off his Phi Slama Jama fame and the mass media attention that Houston's NCAA Championship games garnered, he entered the NBA with a tremendous amount of fanfare. Having performed so well in leading his team to three consecutive NCAA Final Four appearances and a pair of championship game runner-up finishes,

Hakeem was a winner at the collegiate level. But what made him the best prospect in the 1984 NBA Draft was his complete set of skills at the center position. He was a legitimate 7-footer. However, compared to other 7-footers coming into the NBA, Olajuwon already had what they call an "NBA body," as he was listed at about 250 pounds. He wasn't skinny nor was he overly muscular. He was just simply built well with the right amount of lean meat and muscle to compete against the big men in the big league.

Coming out of college, Hakeem Olajuwon was a supreme defensive juggernaut. In his first year of playing college basketball, he averaged merely 18 minutes but was still able to block more than 2 shots per game. As his minutes and his role increased, his defensive prowess was on full display, and he blocked more than 5 shots a game in his final two years in college. Not only was he swatting baskets left and right. Hakeem was also adept at getting his hands on the ball for steals. Besides that, he cleaned up possessions really well with his rebounding skills. Defensively, he was a monster.

Defense was his calling card, but Hakeem Olajuwon was also a refined offensive player. Because of his upbringing as a handball and soccer player, Olajuwon's hand-eye coordination and footwork were more than anyone could ask from a 7-footer. Though he was never really the focal point of offense, he was able to contribute with double-digit scoring in his final two years in college. What made that number impressive was that he was shooting over 60% from the field. Reaching that number is easy if the player dunks the ball all day or waits all night under the basket.

However, Olajuwon posted up a lot of players and scored using his unique combination of skill, athleticism, quickness, and footwork.

Because of that profile mix of size together with refined offensive and defensive skills, Olajuwon entered the 1984 NBA Draft as the consensus overall No. 1 pick in what would ultimately wind up being one of the best draft classes in NBA history. Olajuwon was picked ahead of future Hall-of-Famers Michael Jordan, Charles Barkley, and John Stockton. The 1984 NBA draft is also known in infamy for Portland's selection of oft-injured Kentucky center Sam Bowie with the second overall pick ahead of Jordan, since the Blazers already had a talented guard on their roster in Olajuwon's former Phi Slama Jama teammate Clyde Drexler, who had left college as a junior the year before Olajuwon left.

The 1984 NBA draft was the last one before the NBA lottery was implemented. So a coin flip between the Houston Rockets and Portland Trail Blazers allowed Olajuwon the opportunity to start a new chapter in his basketball life in the city of Houston. The moment also marked just the second time that a University of Houston player had been selected with the No.1 overall draft pick, joining Elvin Hayes in 1968. A coin flip the previous year between Houston and the Indiana Pacers allowed the Rockets to draft 7-foot-4 Virginia athletic big man Ralph Sampson. Now paired with the 7-foot-tall Olajuwon, the two became known as the Twin Towers. A lot was expected of the talented and tall duo of Olajuwon and Sampson. Expectations weighed heavily on the young stars.

## Rookie Season

Though he was the shorter of the Twin Tower duo, Hakeem Olajuwon played center in his rookie season, while Sampson was delegated to the power forward spot. Together, the two 7-footers were unstoppable. In his first game as an NBA player, Olajuwon proved that he was not just a defensive weapon as he scored 24 points against the Dallas Mavericks in a 10-point win. Two games later, he had his first double-double of the season as he piled up 25 points, 13 rebounds, 2 steals, and an amazing 6 blocks in a win versus the Kansas City Kings. He followed that up with two straight double-doubles.

From the end of November up to December 11, 1984, Olajuwon had nine straight games of double-digit rebounding. He could have had nine straight double-doubles had he scored more than 9 points in a win versus the Atlanta Hawks. In two of those games, he went up to grab 19 rebounds. In the second of those, which was a loss to the Los Angeles Clippers, he pulled down 10 offensive rebounds while scoring 30 points. In the next game, he had 42 points, 13 boards, and 5 blocks in a loss to the Golden State Warriors.

On January 15, 1985, Olajuwon had a new career high of 8 blocks in a loss to the Portland Traiblazers. He also had 29 points and 10 boards that night. Four days later, he had his first 30-20 game as he scored 34 points and grabbed a then career-best 20 boards, which included 11 on the offensive end. Because of his exploits as a rookie center, Hakeem Olajuwon was chosen as an All-Star in just his first season in the league.

Shortly after the All-Star break, Hakeem went for his second 30-20 game. He scored 30 points and grabbed a new career-high 25 rebounds, including 15 offensive boards, in a win over the New York Knicks. That was the fifth straight game of five consecutive double-double outings. He grabbed 25 rebounds again in a loss to the Denver Nuggets on March 5. In that game, he also blocked 7 shots. Two weeks after that one, he had 21 boards in a win over Michael Jordan's Chicago Bulls.

Though he carried a lot of expectations, Olajuwon was able to handle them. He finished second to Jordan in the Rookie of the Year Award balloting. Olajuwon averaged 20.6 points, 11.9 rebounds, 1.2 steals, and 2.7 blocks. He was vital in helping the Rockets make a dramatic turnaround from a 29-53 record the previous season to a 48-34 mark and a berth in the playoffs. Hakeem Olajuwon was named to the NBA All-Rookie Team and also to the NBA All-Defensive Second Team. He finished fourth in rebounding and second in blocks. He had nine games in which he scored more than 30 points. He also scored 20 or more points on four different occasions while also blocking 8 shots three different times. Olajuwon and his new Twin Towers teammate Sampson combined to become the first teammates to both average more than 20 points and 10 rebounds since Wilt Chamberlain and Elgin Baylor achieved the milestone in 1970.

In the first round of Hakeem's first trip to the playoffs, the Houston Rockets faced the Utah Jazz. After dropping Game 1 by 14, Olajuwon helped his team win Game 2 by 26 points. He had 16 points and 10 rebounds in that game. Despite losing Game 3, he had 26 points, 16 boards, 5 steals, and 2 blocks. The Rockets extended the series by winning Game 4. However, they ended up biting the dust as the Jazz beat them in Game 5. Hakeem Olajuwon had 32 points, 14 rebounds, and 6 blocks in that game. Throughout the five-game playoff exit, Olajuwon averaged 21 points, 13 rebounds, and 2.6 blocks. All five games were double-double outings for The Dream.

**First Finals Appearance**

The dream would not stop for Hakeem Olajuwon as he entered his second season in the NBA. Though he had finished second to Sampson in scoring for the Houston Rockets in his rookie season, Hakeem developed into the team's deadliest offensive option in his sophomore season as a professional.

Olajuwon scored 27 points and grabbed 11 rebounds in his first game of the 1985-86 season. He followed up that performance with three more consecutive double-doubles. In the last game of that stretch, he had 30 points and 19 rebounds against the Sacramento Kings. Two games later, he grabbed 11 offensive boards for a total of 18 rebounds together with 41 points in a big win versus Portland. It was a good start for the year for Hakeem as he had 16 double-doubles in his first 20 games; 11 of those games were 20-10 performances on points and rebounds.

For the month of December alone, Hakeem Olajuwon had three games of 10 or more offensive rebounds as he further cemented his name as one of the best glass cleaners in the NBA. In the same month, he had eight 20-10 games, which included five straight outings with those numbers. On January 7, 1986, Hakeem Olajuwon posted his first career triple-double. While most players have triple-doubles on points, assists, and rebounds, The Dream did it by blocking a lot of shots. He had 26 points, 12 rebounds, and a then career-high 11 blocks. He also had 7 assists that night. Had

Hakeem assisted on three more baskets, he would have recorded a rare quadruple-double.

For the second straight season, Hakeem Olajuwon was selected as an All-Star for the Western Conference squad. However, he missed a bunch of games after the midseason classic because of injuries. Nevertheless, he made his return a month later and played merely 22 minutes in a big win against the Los Angeles Clippers. Shortly after coming back, he had his first 30-20 game of the season with 33 points and 23 rebounds. He also had 7 steals and 4 blocks in that game. Two games later, he grabbed 21 boards while blocking 8 shots and scoring 27 in a win at Indiana.

While he pulled down merely 9 rebounds in a loss to Detroit a game later, he posted two straight games of 20 or more rebounds. He had 17 points and 20 boards against the Washington Bullets on March 29. Hakeem followed that up with 34 points, 22 rebounds, 5 assists, 4 steals, and 7 blocks against the Golden State Warriors. He then finished strong with two double-doubles in the final two games of the regular season.

At the end of the regular season, Hakeem Olajuwon's numbers saw improvement. He averaged 23.5 points, 11.5 rebounds, 2 steals, and 3.4 blocks. Olajuwon was named to the All-NBA Second Team. He also had 46 double-doubles. One of those games included a rare triple-double for a big man. He led the Houston Rockets to a record of 51 wins as against 31 losses. In the 66 games he played, Hakeem contributed to 44 wins. The Rockets were the second seed in the Western Conference bracket.

Hakeem Olajuwon and the Rockets stamped their name as one of the top teams in the postseason as they swept the Sacramento Kings in the first round. Hakeem had 29 points, 15 rebounds, and 4 blocks in the opening game. After a pedestrian performance marred by foul trouble in Game 2, he finished with 14 points and 13 rebounds as Houston finished off their foes in three easy games.

In Game 1 of their second-round showdown versus the Denver Nuggets, Hakeem Olajuwon turned in one of his best playoff performances. He had 38 points, 16 rebounds, 4 assists, 6 steals, and 5 blocks in the 7-point win. He then scored 18 points and had 14 boards in an 18-point win in

Game 2. Despite another great output from Hakeem, who had 31 points, 11 rebounds, 5 steals, and 7 blocks in Game 3, the Nuggets won the third game by a mere point and tied the series by winning Game 4. The Rockets got back to form, winning Game 5 by 28 points. Olajuwon had 36 points and 19 rebounds, which included 10 offensive boards. He then scored 28 as his team moved past the Nuggets to get to the Western Conference finals.

In the Western finals, Hakeem Olajuwon went head-to-head with Kareem Abdul-Jabbar, a man also regarded as one of the best centers the world has ever seen. Olajuwon had 28 points, 16 rebounds, and 4 blocks in that game versus 31 points by Abdul-Jabbar. The Lakers won by 12 points. As Hakeem scored 22 points, grabbed 13 rebounds, and blocked 6 shots in Game 2, the Rockets stole home-court advantage with a big 10-point win.

The series shifted over to Houston for Games 3 and 4 and the Rockets did not let up. Hakeem Olajuwon scored a playoff career-high 40 points to go along with 12 boards in an 8-point win. He followed that up with 35 points and 4 blocks as the Rockets went up 3-1 with a win in Game 4.

As the Rockets were smelling a trip to the finals, the defending champion Lakers fought hard to keep the title in Los Angeles. However, Hakeem had his third straight great game, scoring 30 points and blocking 4 shots in a tight 2-point victory. With that win, Hakeem Olajuwon was on his way to the NBA finals for the first time in his career.

In the NBA finals, Hakeem went up against another great NBA center, Robert "The Chief" Parish, one of the three players known as the Celtic Big Three. Though Olajuwon outplayed his matchup in Game 1, scoring 33 points and pulling down 12 rebounds, the Celtics came out with a 12-point win. Despite playing tough defense on The Chief, The Dream and his team ended up losing Game 2 by 22 points. The Rockets were down 0-2, and were desperate for a win so as not to go down three losses to no wins.

The Rockets closed in on the Boston Celtics by winning Game 3 at home. Hakeem Olajuwon had 23 points while Sampson had 24 markers and 22 boards. They came out with a 2-point win. Despite a valiant fight in Game 4, the Rockets could not protect their home court, as the Celtics won by 3 points. Olajuwon was limited to 38% shooting that night, as he scored 20 points and grabbed 14 rebounds. While the Rockets extended the series to one more game thanks to the 32 points, 14 rebounds, and 8 blocks of The Dream in Game 5, the Boston Celtics ultimately won the NBA championship with a big win in Game 6.

## Fall From the Top

The defending Western Conference champions experienced a mini fall-off in the 1986-87 season. That was not because Olajuwon was slacking off. If anything, he had to pick up the pieces of the Rockets in that season. The fall was because of the lingering knee injuries that Ralph Sampson was facing. The first skyscraper of the Twin Towers was beginning to collapse. Thankfully, Hakeem's foundations were as strong as ever.

Olajuwon started his third season by scoring 26 points, grabbing 17 rebounds, and blocking 6 shots in the opening win against the Los Angeles Lakers in a rematch of their West finals bout. Hakeem followed up with 26 points and 11 boards against the Kings. After that, he had 31 points, 17 rebounds, 3 steals, and 5 blocks in a tight loss to the Clippers. Olajuwon then had a phenomenal stat line of 25 points, 20 rebounds (with 10 on the offensive board), 6 assists, 4 steals, and 4 blocks against the Kings once again in a 12-point win. He then put up two more double-doubles to make it six straight at the start of the 1986-87 season.

On December 16, 1986, Hakeem went for more than 20 rebounds once again, as he had 24 points and 21 rebounds, including 10 offensive boards, in a loss to Phoenix. On January 10, 1987, he had 20 rebounds yet again, including 10 offensive boards, to go along with 25 points, 2 steals, and 3 blocks against the Dallas Mavericks. That was the middle game of six straight double-double performances. From the end of January up to early February, Hakeem Olajuwon had seven straight double-double games, highlighted by a near triple-double on February 5 as he had 9 blocks in a game versus the Golden State Warriors.

Hakeem Olajuwon went on to play in his third straight All-Star Game. He continued to play like a beast after the midseason classic. About a month later, he completed another triple-double by posting an amazing stat line. On March 10, Hakeem had 38 points, 17 rebounds, 6 assists, 7 steals, and a new career-high 12 blocks. Had he assisted on four more baskets and stolen three more balls, Hakeem Olajuwon could have been the first and only player to have five major statistical categories in double digits.

In his third NBA season, Hakeem Olajuwon averaged 23.4 points, 11.4 rebounds, 2.9 assists, 1.9 steals, and 3.4 blocks. He had a total of 52 double-doubles, which included one triple-double. He was named to the All-NBA First Team and the All-Defensive First Team. Olajuwon kept the boat floating with Sampson limited to merely 43 games in that entire season. The Rockets were the sixth seed in the Western Conference heading into the postseason with a record of 42-40.

Olajuwon opened the first-round series against the Portland Trailblazers with 30 points, 10 rebounds, 6 assists, 4 steals, and 5 blocks as the Rockets defeated the team of his old buddy, Clyde Drexler. The Blazers bounced back with a 13-point win in Game 2. Hakeem then had another amazing game, recording 31 points, 11 boards, and 8 blocks in a Game 3 win. The Rockets closed out the Blazers with a 12-point win in Game 4, as The Dream had 27 points, 9 rebounds, 5 assists, 4 steals, and 5 blocks.

The Rockets met a roadblock named the Seattle SuperSonics in the second round of the playoffs. Despite two good performances of their superstar, the Rockets dropped the first two games. Olajuwon had 28 points and 16 boards in Game 1 and then 27 and 13 in Game 2. His numbers produced dividends in Game 3 as The Dream had 33 points, 11 rebounds, and 4 blocks in a big 18-point win.

The two foes split the next two games as the Sonics went up 3-2 in the series. In a Game 5 win, Hakeem Olajuwon had 26 points, 6 rebounds, and 7 blocks. Hakeem fought hard to force two overtimes in Game 6 as his team was merely one loss away from elimination. In that epic game, Olajuwon had 49 points to go along with a career-high 25 rebounds, including 11 on the offensive end. He also blocked 6 shots. Unfortunately, the Sonics escaped that double-overtime classic by 3 points. With that, the Houston Rockets were eliminated without having been able to defend their Western Conference title.

## Becoming the Lone Tower, Several First-Round Exits

As Ralph Sampson, the first tower of Houston's 7-footer duo, could not get back to his All-Star form because of his knee injuries, the Rockets leaned even more on Hakeem Olajuwon during the 1987-88 season. As the early season passed and Sampson's foundations just could not take the grind anymore, the Houston Rockets decided to trade their prized skyscraper to the Golden State Warriors. Sampson only played 19 games in the season. Thus, the Twin Towers era of the Houston Rockets ended after merely three seasons.

Despite the loss of his front court partner, Hakeem Olajuwon was still in prime form as he led the Rockets. Olajuwon started the new season with six straight double-doubles. Houston was 5-1 in that stretch. On November 19, 1987, Hakeem had an amazing game on both ends of the court in a win over the Cleveland Cavaliers. He had 27 points and 11 rebounds. What made that game amazing was the fact that The Dream also had 8 steals and 5 blocks. You seldom see guards getting 8 steals in a game. Seeing a huge 7-footer getting that many pilfers is just unfair by any standard. That's how amazing Hakeem Olajuwon was on the defensive end of the floor.

On December 10, he had a similar outing, as he poured in 19 points, with 14 rebounds, 4 steals, and 7 blocks. Two games later, he started a seven-game double-double streak. In one of those games, he had 24 points, 14 rebounds, 5 assists, 4 steals, and 6 blocks. As the new year started, Hakeem did not slow down. He had his first 30-20 game of the season on January 7, 1988, with 30 points, 20 rebounds, and 6 blocks. The following game, he had 33 points, 16 rebounds, 5 steals, and 2 blocks.

In a big win over the Indiana Pacers on January 16, Olajuwon had his second game with 20 or more rebounds; he had 25 points and 20 boards. He was then selected to his fourth straight All-Star Game. Shortly after that break, he had 20 points and 20 rebounds in a loss to the Lakers on February 18. He then had 28 points, 20 rebounds, and 6 steals in a loss to Portland. That was the last in an eight-game double-double streak.

Near the end of the season, Hakeem had a nine-game double-double stretch. In that streak, he had 29 points, 21 rebounds, 4 steals, and 5 blocks in a win over the Portland Trailblazers. Then, in a loss versus the Spurs, he had a triple-double in a bad way as he had 26 points, 20 rebounds, and 10 turnovers. Versus the same team barely two weeks later, he had another triple-double, with 38 points, 10 rebounds, 4 assists, 5 steals, and 10 blocks. However, the Rockets lost that one, too.

For the season, Hakeem Olajuwon averaged 22.8 points, 12.1 rebounds, 2.1 steals, and 2.7 blocks. He was once again named to the All-NBA First Team as he had already established himself as the NBA's best center. He was also a member of the All-Defensive First Team. What was amazing about Hakeem's season was that he finished in the top 10 in four major statistical categories (points, rebounds, steals, and blocks). The Rockets ended with a record of 46-36, which was good enough for the sixth seed once again.

In the first round of the playoffs, the Rockets squared off against the Dallas Mavericks. In Game 1, Hakeem had 34 points and 14 rebounds, but the output came in a loss. He then bounced back to lead Houston to an 11-point win in Game 2. He had one of his best playoff games, as he posted 41 points, 26 rebounds, 3 steals, and 4 blocks. Despite 35 points and 12 rebounds from the NBA's finest center, the Rockets lost Game 3. Olajuwon posted great numbers of 40 points and 15 boards yet again in Game 4. However, the team lost that one and bowed out of the playoffs much earlier than they would have wanted. Hakeem was a one-man show, averaging 37.5 points, 16.8 rebounds, 2.3 steals, and 2.8 blocks in the four postseason games.

Despite starting the 1988-89 season without his partner Ralph Sampson, Hakeem had several other teammates ready to pick up the cudgels. Sleepy Floyd, who was part of the trade that sent Sampson to the Warriors, played an integral role in running the offense around Olajuwon. The front court was bolstered with the arrival of Otis Thorpe. Though Thorpe was not the big presence that Sampson was, he brought the same kind of scoring and rebounding punch that the 7'4" former Rocket brought. That was a team ready to make a dent in the playoffs.

Hakeem started the 1988-89 season with a bang. He had back-to-back 30-point games at the start of the regular season: 39 points and 19 rebounds against Denver, and 33 points, 15 boards, 5 steals, and 6 blocks versus Dallas. However, both games were losses. Nevertheless, Houston won seven of their next eight games with Olajuwon playing like Olajuwon.

From November 19 up to November 23, 1988, Hakeem had three great defensive games together with amazing stats. He had 34 points, 12 rebounds, 4 steals, and 6 blocks against the Pistons in an 11-point win. He then had 19 points, 14 rebounds, 3 steals, and 6 blocks in a win over the Atlanta Hawks. Finally, The Dream had 31 points, 14 rebounds, and 7 blocks versus the Utah Jazz in a loss. Two games later, he narrowly missed a triple-double as he recorded 18 points, 15 rebounds, and 9 blocks in a win against the Golden State Warriors.

From December 2 up to January 26, 1989, Hakeem Olajuwon posted 11 straight double-doubles. He had 15 or more rebounds in seven of those games. On top of that, Hakeem had multiple blocks in nine of those 11 outings.

The Rockets were 8-3 in that stretch. It goes to show that the Houston Rockets went as far as Olajuwon could take them with his amazing play on both ends of the court.

For the fifth straight season since his rookie year, Hakeem was selected to play in the All-Star Game as part of the Western Conference squad. Shortly after the midseason break, he had 29 points and 25 rebounds in a narrow loss against Patrick Ewing and the New York Knicks. After that outing, he started an 11-game streak of double-doubles on February 27. The streak ended on March 16. In the middle of that amazing stretch, he had 29 points and 22 rebounds versus the Dallas Mavericks in a win. He then had a 40-20 game as he scored 40 points and grabbed 24 rebounds in a tough loss to the Sacramento Kings. He had 36 points and 23 rebounds one game after his 11-game streak ended.

Hakeem Olajuwon ended the season with a 12-game double-double streak. In the second game of that streak, he barely missed a triple-double, as he had 29 points, 12 rebounds, and 9 assists. Two games later, he had 43 points, 13 rebounds, 8 steals, and 5 blocks. Hakeem Olajuwon was simply all over the floor as he often scored, rebounded, and defended at a high level every single game.

Olajuwon averaged 24.8 points, a league-leading 13.5 rebounds, 2.6 steals, and 3.4 blocks. For the second straight season, he was in the top 10 in points, rebounds, steals, and blocks, becoming the first player to do that in back-to-back seasons. He was named to the All-NBA First Team for the third straight season as he led the Houston Rockets to a record of 45-37, which gave them the fifth seed in the Western Conference playoff bracket.

In the first round, the Rockets faced the Seattle SuperSonics. Personally, Hakeem did not disappoint. as he posted 28 points, 9 boards, 5 assists, 3 steals, and 2 blocks in the opening game. However, his team ended up losing that one. Despite another good performance from the NBA's best center, the Sonics still won Game 2. With the rest of the Rockets clicking on all cylinders in Game 3, Houston managed to get a lone victory in Game 3. Olajuwon had 19 points, 18 rebounds, 4 assists, and 6 blocks in that game. He posted another good double-double in Game 4. But his efforts went in vain as Seattle proceeded to the second round with a four-game series win against the Rockets.

If you think Olajuwon had already peaked at an individual level in the 1988-89 season, think again as he continued his dominating ways into the 1989-90 season. Despite a slow first game, Hakeem picked up the cudgels soon after. He had two 20-rebound games in just his first five games of the season. He posted 13 points and 20 rebounds in a 23-point win versus Portland on November 7, 1989, and he followed that performance two games later with his first triple-double of the season with 24 points, 21 rebounds, and 12 assists. Hakeem also had 5 steals in that outing.

On December 12, Olajuwon narrowly missed another triple-double, as he posted 25 points, 20 rebounds, and 9 blocks in a blowout win versus the Phoenix Suns. Five days later, he completed his second triple-double with a big win versus the Orlando Magic. He finished with 32 points, 25 rebounds, and 10 blocks in that game. Less than a week after that output, he had 29 points, 21 rebounds, 4 steals, and 5 blocks versus the Sacramento Kings in a win.

From December 29 up to January 23, 1990, Olajuwon posted 12 straight double-double games. He had 15 or more rebounds in seven of those outings while also blocking 4 or more shots in eight games. A game after his streak ended, he had 32 points and 20 rebounds in a tough loss to the Mavericks on January 27. That was a start of an 11-game double-double stretch. He also had eight games of blocking 4 or more shots. In the midst of that streak, he was selected to the All-Star Game for the sixth straight season.

On February 27, Hakeem had 37 points, 25 rebounds, and 5 blocks in a loss versus the Detroit Pistons. He bounced back with two consecutive great games. In the next game, against the Suns, he had 41 points, 14 rebounds, and 7 blocks in an 8-point win. As the Rockets defeated the Warriors by 20 points in the next game, Hakeem had a triple-double performance with 29 points, 18 rebounds, and 11 blocks. He missed another opportunity for a quadruple-double as he had 9 assists in that game.

From March 10 up to April 14, Hakeem Olajuwon had 17 straight double-double performances. There were several great games in that stretch. He had 17 points, 22 rebounds, and 8 blocks versus the Kings on March 15. He then had 21 points, 20 rebounds, and 7 assists in a loss to Portland on March 20. Finally, on March 29, Hakeem Olajuwon finished a 26-point win with a rare quadruple-double. He recorded 18 points, 16 rebounds, 10 assists, and 11 blocks. He was only the third player in NBA history at that time to have recorded to a quadruple-double. Only David Robinson had a similar stat line after Olajuwon did it. On April 19, he finished a loss to the Denver Nuggets with 52 points, 18 rebounds, 3 steals, and 3 blocks.

In his sixth season as an NBA player, Hakeem Olajuwon averaged 24.3 points, a league-leading 14 boards, 2.9 assists, 2.1 steals, and an NBA-high 4.6 blocks. He was nominated to the All-NBA Second Team as well as to the All-Defensive First Team. As good a player that Olajuwon was on the individual level, the Houston Rockets struggled to get into the playoffs with a record of 41-41. They were merely the eighth seed heading into the postseason.

In the first round versus the top-seeded LA Lakers, Olajuwon struggled against the defense of Mychal

Thompson and AC Green in the first two games. He only had 13 points in a Game 1 loss, but he did have 14 rebounds and 7 blocks. Olajuwon was then limited to 11 points in Game 2 though he finished with a triple-double with 11 rebounds and 10 blocks. Hakeem finally broke out of the slump as he scored 22 to lead his team to victory in Game 3. And though he scored 28 in Game 4, the Lakers came out with an easy 21-point win. Once again, Hakeem Olajuwon and the Houston Rockets bowed out early from the playoffs.

Hakeem continued to almost singlehandedly carry the Houston Rockets on his shoulders heading into the 1990-91 season. In his first 20 games in the new season, Olajuwon had 17 double-doubles. Of those 17 games, he had nine outings of 15 or more rebounds. Hakeem had four 20-rebound games that early in the season, and he even had two 30-20 games. On the defensive end, he did not let up as he had 10 games of 4 or more blocks. In each of his first 20 games, The Dream had at least one block.

On December 20, 1990, Olajuwon had his first triple-double of the season as he recorded 24 points, 16 rebounds, and 11 blocks. The next game, he pulled down 19 rebounds. The game after that, Hakeem had 25 points, 20 rebounds, and 7 blocks. Those performances came during a 16-game streak of double-doubles. However, on January 3, 1991, Hakeem Olajuwon took a blow to the eye from Bill Cartwright in a game versus the Chicago Bulls. He would miss the rest of that game and the next 25 due to a fractured eye socket.

Hakeem missed the All-Star Game as a result of the injury he suffered at the hands of Cartwright. After his injury, Olajuwon had to wear goggles throughout almost the rest of his career. He returned to the court on February 28, when he recorded 24 points and 16 rebounds in a loss. After that loss, he led the Rockets to a 13-game winning streak. From March 14 to the end of the season, Hakeem Olajuwon had 25 straight double-doubles.

During the regular season, Olajuwon averaged 21.2 points, 13.8 rebounds, 2.2 steals, and 3.9 blocks. Hakeem actually led the NBA in rebounding average. However, since he played only 56 games that season, he could not qualify for the title of rebounding king. Nevertheless, he was the league's best shot blocker and he was named to the All-NBA Third Team and the All-Defensive Second Team. He led the Rockets to a record of 52 wins as against 30 losses. They were the sixth seed in the increasingly competitive Western Conference.

Despite a strong finish to the regular season, the Rockets once again met a quick end in their playoff run at the hands of the Los Angeles Lakers. In the three-game sweep, Hakeem could not score more than 23 points, though he did have double-digit rebounding in all three games. The Dream once again struggled against the defensive prowess of Vlade Divac, AC Green, and Sam Perkins.

## Missing the Playoffs

Hakeem Olajuwon missed the first seven games of the 1991-92 season because of an irregular heartbeat. Despite that, he made a big season debut with 29 points, 18 rebounds, and 5 steals in a win against the LA Lakers. Two games later, he had 27 points, 20 rebounds, and 5 blocks in a win over the Blazers. Olajuwon recorded his first 30-20 game of the season with 33 points and 23 rebounds, plus 5 blocks, in a narrow win over the Golden State Warriors.

From the end of December 1991 to the end of January 1992, Olajuwon had a one-month streak of 17 straight double-doubles. During that stretch, he had back-to-back games of 9 blocks. He narrowly missed triple-doubles in those games. Hakeem also had at least a block in all 17 games. He had nine outings of blocking at least 4 shots. Olajuwon also recorded another 30-20 game in the middle of that streak, as he had 34 points and 23 rebounds in a win against the Minnesota Timberwolves. He returned to the NBA All-Star Game that season.

In his first game after the All-Star break, Hakeem Olajuwon scored 40 points and grabbed 19 boards in a loss to the Seattle SuperSonics. After that game, he flirted with a triple-double again with 17 points, 13 rebounds, and 9 blocks. On February 26, he had a near triple-double once again, but it was in the conventional way as he recorded 33 points, 12 rebounds, and 9 assists in a win against Golden State.

Hakeem averaged 21.6 points, 12.1 rebounds, 1.8 steals, and 4.3 blocks that season. However, he did not garner any mention for the All-NBA and the All-Defensive teams because the Houston Rockets struggled all year long. They could not make the playoffs with a mediocre record of 42 wins versus 40 losses. They even replaced former head coach Don Chaney with former Rocket Rudy Tomjanovich in the middle of the season to try to salvage the year. Had that record been attained several years ago, they would have made the postseason. But, as the 90's began, the Western Conference became tougher than it had ever been. Hakeem's Rockets were quickly folding under the pressure of a competitive conference.

## Improved Offensive Repertoire, Defensive Player of the Year, Return to the Postseason

Several questions arose for Hakeem Olajuwon as he was headed into the 1992-93 season. The frustrations of losing several times in the first round of the playoffs and not even making it into the postseason in 1992 weighed down on Hakeem. He was angry with the Rockets organization for not surrounding him with a good supporting cast. He openly criticized team owner Charlie Thomas for his supposed lack of a desire to win games. With the way things went on with Olajuwon versus the management, many began speculating that a deal to send away Hakeem from Houston was in the works, especially because a contract extension had not been signed at that time.

However, Hakeem Olajuwon was able to mend things with team ownership. He signed an extension with the Rockets on top of earning United States citizenship via naturalization. On the other hand, the team gave Rudy Tomjanovich the full-time job of coaching the team. The new contract and the repaired relationship between Olajuwon and team management led to a breakout year for the man who was already widely regarded as the best center in the whole NBA.

Olajuwon did not disappoint his team owner as he started the 1992-93 season with 13 straight double-doubles. While it may sound a little farfetched, Hakeem was able to rebound and score more because he passed the ball a lot more. With opposing defenses unable to focus on him, Hakeem was free to roam the paint to score points and grab more rebounds. On top of all that, his defense never wavered. In just his first five games of the season, he had already totaled 29 blocks. Throughout his first 20 games, he blocked r or more shots on 14 times. The Dream was simply a beast in all facets of the game.

On January 3, 1993, Hakeem Olajuwon barely missed a triple-double as he recorded 40 points, 9 rebounds, and 10 blocks. Two weeks later, he had 42 points, 12 rebounds, 6 assists, and 3 blocks in a win against Patrick Ewing's Knicks. Five days later, he scored 38 points to go along with 8 rebounds, 4 assists, and 7 blocks. The Rockets were in the middle of a seven-game streak that time after losing seven straight outings.

With The Dream healthy and still playing at a superstar's level, he was selected to play in his eighth All-Star Game. After the midseason classic, Hakeem led the Rockets to 15 straight victories. In that streak of wins, he had 13 double-doubles and eight games in which he blocked 4 or more shots. His passing wasn't too bad either, as he had 5 or more assists in eight games during that stretch.

After that 15-game streak ended, Olajuwon led his team to 11 straight wins with the season winding down. He had several terrific games during that streak. Hakeem recorded

38 points, 19 rebounds, 5 assists, and 4 blocks on April 3. He followed that up with 42 points, 13 rebounds, 6 assists, 5 steals, and 4 blocks against the LA Clippers. Two games later, he had 45 points, 14 rebounds, and 4 steals versus David Robinson and the San Antonio Spurs.

By the end of that breakout season, Hakeem Olajuwon averaged a then career-high 26.1 points, 13 rebounds, a then career-high 3.5 assists, 1.8 steals, and 4 blocks. He also upped his field goal percentage to 52.9%, which was his highest since posting 53.8% in his rookie season. His increased scoring clip was a result of a new and improved repertoire on offense. Olajuwon was not merely relying on his athletic ability, but he had also perfected his post moves and his face-up game. That season, Olajuwon was named the Defensive Player of the Year for the first time and he was second to Charles Barkley in the voting for Most Valuable Player. That coincided with his return to the All-NBA First Team as well as to the All-Defensive First Team. He led the Rockets to the second seed in the Western Conference with a record of 55-27.

In the first round of the playoffs, the Rockets met the Los Angeles Clippers. Though the Clippers were never a very competitive team in those days, they were able to push Houston to the brink of another first-round elimination. In Game 1, the Rockets managed to win by 23 with the help of Hakeem's 28 points, 11 rebounds, 6 assists, 4 steals, and 9 blocks. Despite a similar outing in Game 2, the Clippers ended up winning.

Olajuwon upped his scoring in Game 3 as he posted 32 points together with 12 rebounds and 4 blocks. His efforts got the Houston Rockets the victory. However, the Clippers fought back to force Game 5, although Hakeem had amazing numbers of 25 points, 18 rebounds, 9 assists, and 5 blocks in Game 4. The Dream topped off that performance by leading the Rockets to the second round with a 4-point victory in Game 5. He had 31 points, 21 rebounds, 3 steals, and 7 blocks in the deciding game.

Despite playing on a high after getting past the first round for the first time in several years, the Houston Rockets were quickly brought down to earth by the Seattle Sonics, who won Games 1 and 2 of their second-round meeting.

The losses, however, were not because of a lack of effort on Hakeem. He had double-doubles and 5 blocks in each of the two losses. The Rockets took revenge by winning the next two games on their home floor. Olajuwon had double-doubles in both games. He also had 8 blocks in Game 4.

The Rockets and the Sonics split the next two games as they went on to a deciding Game 7 to settle who goes on to the Western Conference finals. Hakeem posted 20 points and 10 rebounds in Game 5, but the Sonics came out winning that one. Though he was limited to 14 points, his lowest in that postseason, Olajuwon's Rockets got a 13-point win to force Game 7. Hakeem and his team fought valiantly in Game 7. The Dream had 23 points, 17 rebounds, 9 assists, and 3 blocks. However, the Sonics were just too tough to get rid off as they went on to win the game by merely 3 points. Though the Houston Rockets could not get as deep into the postseason as they would have wanted, it was still a great return to the playoffs in one of Hakeem's best seasons.

## First Season MVP, Second DPOY, First NBA Title, First Finals MVP

During the 1993-94 season, Hakeem Olajuwon proved that he hadn't peaked yet as he continued to play better than ever before. The Dream continued to live on and his offensive arsenal continued to grow. It was in that season when Hakeem Olajuwon perfected his weapon called "The Dream Shake," which was Hakeem's go-to-move in the peak of his career. It was what made him the best center of his generation.

Sounding more like something you would order with a cheeseburger and fries, Olajuwon's Dream Shake typically began with him holding the ball in the post, followed by a sudden pivot. With his back to his opponent, Olajuwon could turn left and shoot, turn right and shoot, fake one way and shoot the other, or drive straight to the hoop with the defender reeling. While Olajuwon executed individual moves within the "Shake" to perfection, it was the bevy of possibilities and countermoves that really befuddled his opponents, who could never be quite sure which direction he would twist or turn or if he would go toward the hoop or make the pass. It was the most unguardable weapon in the NBA during the 90's.

Hakeem Olajuwon used his perfected offensive weapon to good effect at the start of the 1993-94 season. He had 15 double-doubles in his first 20 games. In the same stretch of games, Hakeem had four games of scoring 30 or more points as well as 14 games with 4 or more blocks. He was the perfect two-way player in the frontcourt, as his offense was just as polished as his defense. Olajuwon even had 16 games with at least 1 steal in his first 20 outings. What was even more amazing was the fact that the Houston Rockets were 15-0 to start the season. At that time, that was the best start in NBA history. It stood as the best undefeated start for over two decades until the Golden State Warriors broke it in 2015.

Olajuwon led the Houston Rockets to a record of 22-3 through their first 25 games. Though the Rockets slowed down a bit during December, Hakeem never got tired of doing what he did best—everything. From December 14, 1993, up until January 18, 1994, Olajuwon had a 16-game streak of double-double performances. He turned in several great individual outings in that stretch. Hakeem had 35 points, 17 rebounds, and 4 blocks in a loss to Denver in the middle of December. He then had back-to-back games of 34 points and 10 rebounds against Seattle and Minnesota. Against the Timberwolves, he also had 5 steals and 8 blocks. Those were two of his four 30-10 games in scoring and rebounding. On January 5, he had 37 points, 14 rebounds, 8 assists, and 3 steals in a win over the Mavericks. A little more than a week later, Olajuwon posted 45 points and 10 rebounds in a loss to the Washington Bullets.

A week after scoring 45 points, Hakeem Olajuwon scored 40 in a win against the Utah Jazz. Though he had a poor shooting night in the following game against the Cleveland Cavaliers, Olajuwon still came out with the win for his team as he had a near triple-double of 13 points, 10 rebounds, and 9 assists. He also had 6 steals and 4 blocks in that game. Hakeem continued to play at a monstrous level as he was selected to his ninth All-Star Game in 10 years. About a month after the midseason classic, Hakeem poured in 41 points, with 13 rebounds and 6 assists versus the Portland Trailblazers. Olajuwon finished the season strong with 12 games of scoring 30 or more points from March until the end of the regular season.

As the regular season ended, there was no doubt that Hakeem Olajuwon was the finest center the NBA had ever seen in that era. He averaged a then career-high 27.3 points, 11.9 rebounds, a career-high 3.6 assists, 1.6 steals, and 3.7 blocks. For the first and only time in his career, Hakeem Olajuwon was named the NBA's Most Valuable Player. For the second straight season, he won the Defensive Player of the Year award. Hakeem Olajuwon became only the second player since Michael Jordan did it in 1988 to have won the MVP and the DPOY in the same season. Along with those awards, Olajuwon saw his name on the All-NBA and All-Defensive First Teams. He led the Rockets to a record of 58-24, which was second best in the West that season.

The newly minted MVP continued his dominating ways in the playoffs. In Game 1 of their first-round meeting with the Portland Trailblazers, Hakeem had 26 points, 10 rebounds, 6 assists, and 6 blocks in a 10-point win. He then led the Rockets to an 11-point win in Game 2 as he recorded 46 points, 8 rebounds, 4 assists, and 6 blocks. Despite another great game, Olajuwon and his Rockets failed to sweep the Blazers in Game 3. Nevertheless, they completed the series win thanks to 36 points and 16 rebounds from The Dream.

In the second round, the Houston Rockets met the Charles Barkley-led Phoenix Suns. Hakeem Olajuwon posted back-to-back games of scoring 30 or more points and pulling down 15 or more rebounds. But the Suns won both closely-fought games. They were looking to complete a sweep by winning both of their home games at Phoenix. But the Houston Rockets had other plans as they were aiming for revenge.

Houston won both games in Phoenix by double digits. In Game 3, Olajuwon had 26 points, 15 rebounds, 6 assists, and 6 blocks. He followed that up with 28 points, 12 rebounds, 8 assists, and 5 blocks in Game 4. The Houston Rockets completed the comeback by defeating the Phoenix Suns in three straight games. Hakeem scored 20 points as the Rockets blew the Suns out of Game 5 with a 23-point win. Phoenix extended the series to seven games by winning Game 6. In Game 7, Olajuwon showed why he was the best player in the NBA at that time. He posted 37 points and 17 rebounds as he led his team to the Western Conference finals with a 10-point win in Game 7.

In the Western Conference finals, the Houston Rockets easily defeated the Utah Jazz in five games even though their opponents had Karl Malone, who was widely regarded as the best power forward of that era and arguably the second best player of the 1990s (next to Jordan). Hakeem scored 31 to take Game 1 by 12. He then poured in 41 points, with 13 rebounds and 6 assists as he and the Rockets moved to take the 2-0 lead over the Jazz. Utah won Game 3 by 9 points, but the Rockets won Games 4 and 5 to proceed to the NBA finals. Olajuwon combined for only 38 points and 19 rebounds in the final two games of the series; both wins were attributable to Houston's much-improved team play.

With that series win over the Utah Jazz, Hakeem Olajuwon was on his way back to the NBA finals, a stage he had not played on since 1986. In the finals, he was tasked to face the New York Knicks led by Patrick Ewing. It was going to be an epic battle between two of the best two-way centers the NBA had in that era. Both players were in their prime, which meant that it was going to be a very entertaining matchup.

In a very defense-oriented final series, Hakeem outplayed Patrick in Game 1 as the Rockets won by 7 points. Olajuwon had 28 points and 10 rebounds while Ewing had 23 points and 9 boards. Hakeem, though he outplayed Ewing in Game 2, could not complete the home-court defense, as the Knicks won that game by 8 points. Houston regained home-court advantage by beating the Knicks in New York by merely 4 points. Olajuwon had 21 points, 11 rebounds, 7 assists, and 7 blocks in that game, and he limited Ewing to 9 out of 29 shooting from the field.

Winning two games in New York proved to be a difficult task as the Knicks won Game 4 by 9 to tie the series. Hakeem had 32 points and 5 blocks in that game and he defended Patrick to perfection once again. Ewing was limited to 8 out of 28 in that game. The Knicks took the series lead by winning Game 5. In that game, it was Patrick

Ewing who got the best of The Dream as he had 25 points, 12 rebounds, and 8 blocks while Olajuwon had 27 points and 8 boards.

Olajuwon's saved his championship hopes with the biggest play of the 1994 NBA finals. With the Rockets leading 86 to 84, the Knicks had possession of the basketball for the final play. John Starks rose up to shoot a three-pointer that could have won the game and the NBA championship. However, Olajuwon poured in all of his defensive abilities to cover Starks and block that shot to preserve the win for the Rockets. Hakeem had 30 points, 10 rebounds, and 4 blocks in that game. In Game 7, Houston outscored the Knicks in all four quarters to win the game and the championship by 6 points. Hakeem Olajuwon finished with 25 points, 10 rebounds, 7 assists, and 3 blocks in that game. Olajuwon won the battle with Ewing by averaging 26.9 points on 50% shooting versus Patrick's 18.9 points on a little over 36% shooting. It was a testament to how great a defender Olajuwon was as he hoisted his first NBA title.

Because of his efforts in the entire 1994 playoffs, Hakeem Olajuwon was named the NBA Finals MVP. He is the only player in the history of the NBA to have ever won the regular-season MVP, the Finals MVP, and the Defensive Player of the Year in the same season. And because of how amazing the Rockets were in winning the NBA championship, Houston was nicknamed "Clutch City" primarily due to their many clutch plays on their path to the richest prize in basketball.

With that NBA title in hand along with the MVP, the Finals MVP, and the DPOY, Hakeem Olajuwon had already established himself not only as the best center in the NBA at that time, but as one of the best, if not the best, centers in league history. What made him great was that he achieved all of those accolades against some of the top centers in NBA history. It was the golden age of centers, as guys like Ewing, Robinson, and Mutombo were all in their prime years, and yet could not beat Olajuwon in their matchups. Even younger centers like Alonzo Mourning and the great Shaquille O'Neal, who was bigger and more athletic than Olajuwon, could not stop The Dream from coming true. You could even say that Hakeem was the best big man of that era as he continuously beat Karl Malone,

Dennis Rodman, and Charles Barkley in achievements and numbers. Against that kind of competition, it's not farfetched to say that Hakeem Olajuwon, at that time, was the best center the NBA has ever seen.

## Second NBA Championship

Hakeem Olajuwon had established himself as the NBA's best center in that era with a championship victory in 1994. He was an MVP and a Finals MVP. So what was left to prove? What was left for him to do? The ordinary player would just sit back and let his career end on cruise control. But Olajuwon was not that kind of a player. He was a consummate competitor who was not contented with one win. He wanted more.

Hakeem started the season on a good note. While he had mediocre games (for a Hakeem Olajuwon) in his first two outings, he put up seven straight double-double performances. On November 9, 1994, he had 43 points, 16 rebounds, and 8 blocks to lead the Rockets past the Indiana Pacers. He led the Rockets to a 9-0 start. On December 1, Hakeem had his first and only triple-double of the season as he posted 37 points, 13 rebounds, and 12 assists in a win over the Golden State Warriors.

On December 29, Hakeem had his second game with 40 or more points when he exploded for 42 in a win against the Warriors. He followed that performance with 37 points, 12 rebounds, 7 assists, and 3 blocks against the Jazz. After that output, he had 41 points, 13 rebounds, and 5 blocks in a win in Dallas. He ended that four-game stretch with 33 points against the Mavs in back-to-back wins against the Dallas-based team.

On January 13 and 14 of 1995, Hakeem Olajuwon had back-to-back games with 40 or more points in a span of 24 hours. He had 47 points, 10 rebounds, and 3 blocks in a win against David Robinson and the Spurs. He followed that by scoring 41 in a losing effort against the Denver Nuggets. On February 2, he went over 40 again, as he scored 41 in a 20-point win over the Jazz. For the 10th time in his 11-year career, the 32-year old Hakeem Olajuwon was selected to play in the All-Star Game.

However, the championship hangover was quick to strike the Houston Rockets, as they struggled to gather enough wins to get a good record in their quest to defend their titles. Olajuwon was playing great as usual, but his team could not follow. As a result, the Rockets decided to trade Otis Thorpe, arguably their second best player since Ralph Sampson was traded several years past, to acquire Portland's Clyde Drexler, the second best shooting guard of that era and Olajuwon's old college teammate. The two former University of Houston teammates would form a deadly inside-outside duo for the Rockets.

Despite the acquisition of Drexler, the Rockets were still not in prime championship form as the season was winding down. Nevertheless, Hakeem played like the MVP that he was. He scored 40 points together with 13 boards and 5 assists on March 7 in a loss to Phoenix. He then scored 30 or more points in the next two games while leading the Rockets to five straight wins in the middle of March.

During the 1994-95 regular season, Olajuwon posted a personal best 27.8 points together with 10.8 rebounds, 3.5 assists, 1.8 steals, and 3.4 blocks. He was named to the All-

NBA Third Team and the All-Defensive Second Team. He also became the Houston Rockets' all-time leading scorer that season. However, he finished second in the NBA MVP voting to San Antonio center David Robinson. The Rockets finished with a record of 47-35, which gave them the sixth seed in the Western Conference. As a low-seeded team, it was going to be a tough title defense for the Houston Rockets.

In the first round, the Rockets had to face the third-seeded Utah Jazz. Despite scoring 45 points in Game 1, Olajuwon's efforts were in vain as the Jazz drew first blood. The Rockets bounced back as Hakeem scored 27 in Game 2 to help his team win by 14. Utah took back the series lead with a 13-point victory in Game 3. With the odds stacked against him and his team, Olajuwon went into a mode unseen from him before. He scored 40 points in Game 4 to push the series to five games. In Game 5, the defending champions defeated the higher-seeded Jazz team; Hakeem had 33 points, 10 rebounds, and 4 assists.

In the second round, the Rockets were up against Charles Barkley and the Suns again. Much as in their matchup in the previous year's playoffs, Phoenix came out with the first two wins of the series. The Rockets lost those games by an average margin of 23 points. At that point, it seemed like Houston's prospects of defending the title were over. But Hakeem would not let up, as he scored 36 points to lead the Rockets to a 33-point win. He had 38 points and 5 blocks in Game 4, but the Suns raced out to a 3-1 lead with a win.

Hakeem would not fail his team. The Dream had 31 points and 16 rebounds to force at least one more game. In Game 6, he had 30 points, 8 rebounds, 10 assists, and 5 blocks to lead Houston to a 13-point win, forcing an all-important Game 7. Hakeem had 29 points, 11 rebounds, 4 assists, and 5 blocks to lead his team to a slim 1-point win in Game 7. By beating the Phoenix Suns in Game 7, Olajuwon and the Houston Rockets lived up to their nickname of Clutch City by winning three straight games after being down 1-3 in the series.

In the Western Conference finals, Hakeem Olajuwon would go head-to-head with the new MVP, David Robinson, and the top-seeded San Antonio Spurs. It was a battle between the two best centers of the 1990s. Robinson was the younger and fresher big man while Olajuwon was a 32-year old center in the prime of his career. It was going to be another epic matchup between the last two MVP's of the NBA. Unfortunately for Robinson, Olajuwon went into an out-of-body experience in the entire series.

Olajuwon scored 27 points, grabbed 8 rebounds, and assisted on 8 baskets to lead the Rockets to an upset victory in Game 1. He then went on to have 41 points and 16 rebounds in Game 2 as he proved that winning Game 1 was no fluke. The Rockets were up 2-0 in the series at that point. Hakeem scored 43 in Game 3, but the Spurs took that win from them. Limited to 20 points, his lowest in the entire series, Olajuwon could not stop San Antonio from claiming Game 4. But it was all downhill for the Spurs at that point.

Hakeem staked his class to be the better center by taking away Games 5 and 6 from David Robinson and the Spurs. He had 42 points, 9 rebounds, 8 assists, and 5 blocks in Game 5, which Houston won by 21. The Dream then shook off the Spurs and headed to the finals with a five-point win in Game 6. He had 39 points, 17 rebounds, and 5 blocks in that game. Overall, you wouldn't even think that Robinson was the MVP that season because Olajuwon outclassed him in every way.

The Admiral averaged 23.8 points on barely 45% shooting in the series. On the other hand, The Dream averaged 35 points on about 56% shooting from the field. It was a totally dominating performance for Hakeem. It was also during that series that the Dream Shake was in full effect. In one of the most memorable moves in NBA history, Olajuwon faced Robinson up. He drove to the basket and then faked a spin to the baseline. David did not bite on that initial fake. Almost instantaneously after that spin fake, Hakeem pivoted to fake a shot, which did make Robinson bite. After getting The Admiral off his feet, Olajuwon went for an easy basket. That was merely one of the many Dream Shakes that Hakeem put on Robinson during the series. It was a dominant performance by Olajuwon, who even had David Robinson saying that there was no way to solve Hakeem and his Dream Shake.

For the second straight season, Hakeem Olajuwon and the Houston Rockets were headed into the NBA finals. In the championship series, the Rockets faced the Orlando Magic, who were led by another young center named Shaquille O'Neal. O'Neal was the most physically imposing center the NBA has ever seen ever since Wilt Chamberlain. He stood 7'1 and weighed about 325 pounds of beefy muscle. On top of all that, he was athletic and offensively polished at the post. Olajuwon had his hands full as he probably never faced a center as imposing as Shaq.

Facing a second younger center, who was hoping to take away the title of best pivot man from him, Hakeem Olajuwon stamped his class all over O'Neal. He scored 31 points to lead the Houston Rockets to a 2-point win in Game 1. He then scored 34 points to go with 11 rebounds and 4 blocks in Game 2 as he continued to perplex and confuse Shaq with his one-of-a-kind moves. As the series shifted over to Houston for Games 3 and 4, Olajuwon would not stop giving O'Neal nightmares. He had 31 points, 14 rebounds, and 7 assists in Game 3. In Game 4, the Rockets completed the sweep over the Orlando Magic with a 12-point win. In that championship-winning game, Hakeem had 35 points, 15 rebounds, 6 assists, and 3 steals.

For the second straight season, Hakeem Olajuwon and the Houston Rockets were NBA champions. For the second straight season, Hakeem was named the Finals MVP as he dominated Shaquille O'Neal. He averaged 32.8 points, 11.5 boards, and 5.5 assists as against Shaq, who averaged 28 points and 12.5 rebounds. He was so good against the bigger, stronger, younger, and more athletic Shaquille O'Neal that even The Big Diesel would go on to say that Olajuwon was the only center he could not solve. He said that Hakeem's bevy of moves and countermoves often kept him off balance because The Dream had more moves than he could count. Olajuwon was simply a beast in the entire postseason as he averaged 33 points, 10.3 rebounds, 4.5 assists, and 2.8 blocks.

Houston's 1994-95 championship season also featured a few team milestones. No squad had previously defeated four 50-win teams on their way to the NBA championship until Olajuwon and the Rockets took down the Utah Jazz (60-22), Phoenix Suns (59-23), San Antonio Spurs (62-20), and Orlando Magic (57-25). The Rockets also became the first team to win nine road playoff games and seven road games in a row. All of which led to head coach Rudy Tomjanovich's famous "never underestimate the heart of a champion" speech.

## Failure to Three-Peat

With Hakeem Olajuwon and Clyde Drexler leading a Houston Rockets team that featured young and serviceable role players such as Robert Horry, Sam Cassell, and Chucky Brown, the team had all the tools to win one more championship and complete a three-peat. They were still one of the top teams heading into the 1995-96 season especially with Hakeem, at 33 years of age, still playing at his prime level despite advancing in NBA years.

Hakeem, even though he was slowly moving past his best athletic form, was still dominating on both ends of the basketball court. He led the Rockets to 15 wins through their first 20 outings. In that span, he had 10 double-double outings. On November 28, 1995, against the LA Clippers, he had 30 points, 19 rebounds, 6 assists, and 5 blocks. He followed that up with 31 points, 13 rebounds, 5 assists, and 3 blocks in a loss to the Jazz.

On December 13, he had his first triple-double in the regular season with 15 points, 14 rebounds, and 10 blocks in a win over the Vancouver Grizzlies. Then, on December 28, Olajuwon had his second triple-double, against the New Jersey Nets. He had 22 points, 18 rebounds, and 10 assists. In the next game, he had 35 points, 11 rebounds, 6 assists, and 4 blocks in a win over the Dallas Mavericks.

Hakeem was then selected to his 11th All-Star Game appearance. After that, he scored 40 points and grabbed 13 boards when the Rockets beat the Kings on February 19, 1996. Ten days later, he had 42 points, 11 rebounds, and 5 assists versus the Philadelphia 76ers. He had another game of scoring 40 or more against the Vancouver Grizzlies near the end of the regular season. Olajuwon had 42 points and 18 rebounds in a win in Canada. In a loss to the Timberwolves, he went for 46 points, 19 rebounds, 8 assists, and 3 blocks. As the season was winding down, he had his third triple-double of the season against the Mavs.

Hakeem finished that game with 31 points, 13 rebounds, and 10 blocks.

In his 12$^{th}$ NBA season, Hakeem Olajuwon averaged 26.9 points, 10.9 rebounds, 3.6 assists, 1.6 steals, and 2.9 blocks. He was named to the All-NBA Second Team as well as the All-Defensive Second Team. Despite his monstrous play, the Houston Rockets were able to win only 48 of 82 games in the regular season. They made the postseason as the fifth seed in the West.

Olajuwon scored 33 points and stole the ball 5 times as the Rockets won Game 1 of their first-round series versus the Los Angeles Lakers in Magic Johnson's final year as a pro. He was then limited to 18 in a loss in Game 2. However, Hakeem got back to prime form as he scored 30 and 25 in Games 3 and 4 to eliminate the Lakers in the first round of the playoffs.

The defending champions would soon meet a roadblock named the Seattle SuperSonics. For some reason, Hakeem could not get his groove going against the Sonics. In Game 1, he had merely 6 points, as Seattle won the game by 33.

He the scored 17 points on 8-of-21 shooting while grabbing 16 rebounds as the SuperSonics took a 2-0 lead. Hakeem turned in a near triple-double performance in Game 3. He had 24 points, 13 rebounds, and 9 assists. Despite that, Seattle took an insurmountable 3-0 lead. As the Rockets were down 0-3 in the series, they fought their way to overtime in Game 4. However, the Seattle Sonics were still the ones who came out with the win as they swept the Houston Rockets in four games. With that loss, it appeared that Hakeem was far below the form he displayed back in the 1995 playoffs. It would also appear that he might have poured all he had in the past year's postseason.

## Reinforced by Barkley, the Houston Big Three

Though Olajuwon's summer started earlier than he had hoped, the 1996 offseason featured a few memorable moments in his life. Having gained American citizenship three years earlier, he was named to the U.S. Olympic team that won a gold medal at the Summer Olympic Games in Atlanta. He also received another unique honor in his storied career as he was named one of the 50 Greatest Players in NBA History by the league.

As the 1996-97 season was about to begin, the Houston Rockets made a trade that changed the fate of the team. They sent a package of four respectable players in exchange for the Phoenix Suns' franchise player and former MVP Charles Barkley. With the added reinforcement, the Houston Rockets formed a Big Three of some of the best superstars during the 90's era. They had Clyde Drexler, Charles Barkley, and Hakeem Olajuwon. With that kind of a lineup, the rest of the NBA was put on notice.

With Barkley in the fold, Hakeem Olajuwon no longer needed to do everything. Barkley focused on rebounding and playmaking at the power forward spot. He was also the team's second best scorer. Meanwhile, The Dream focused on scoring and defense. Olajuwon started the season by scoring 30 or more points on five different occasions in the team's first 20 games. He led Houston to a record of 18-2 in those 20 games. In that span, he had seven double-doubles.

Olajuwon continued to score and defend well throughout the season, though his rebounding stats were beginning to fall because of how Barkley manned that part of the game. On January 25, 1997, Hakeem had 41 points, 15 rebounds, and 6 assists versus the Utah Jazz. He followed that performance by scoring 48 points on 24-of-40 shooting from the field. However, both games were losses. Nevertheless, The Dream was selected to play in his 12$^{th}$ and final All-Star Game. On March 4, he had his first and only triple-double of the season as he recorded 22 points, 16 rebounds, and 10 assists.

At the end of the regular season, Hakeem Olajuwon had averaged 23.2 points, 9.2 rebounds, 3 assists, 1.5 steals, and 2.2 blocks. He was named to the All-Defensive Second Team. That was his final appearance at an All-Defensive Team. Because of the new Houston Big Three, the Rockets finished the season with a record of 57-25, which was the third-best record in the Western Conference.

As the postseason got started, the Houston Big Three were in prime form against their first-round opponents. They easily defeated the Minnesota Timberwolves, who were led by a young upstart named Kevin Garnett. The Rockets blew the Wolves out in the first two games before winning the third game by 5 points. In that three-game sweep, Olajuwon averaged 18.3 points and 10.3 rebounds.

In the second round, they faced the Seattle Sonics, the team that had eliminated them in the previous postseason. The Rockets were looking to get revenge against the team that denied them a three-peat. Olajuwon contributed 15 points and 11 rebounds in a win in Game 1. Despite similar numbers from the superstar center, the SuperSonics got away with a close win in Game 2. In Game 3, Olajuwon poured in 24 points, 11 rebounds, 4 steals, and 3 blocks to win it by 4 points. In Game 4, he focused on defense and playmaking. He finished the win with 11 points, 12 rebounds, 9 assists, and 3 blocks.

Although the Houston Rockets were leading 3-1 in the series, the Seattle Sonics would not go down so easily. Despite two straight 30-point double-doubles from Hakeem Olajuwon in Games 5 and 6, the Sonics were able to win two consecutive to force Game 7. The Rockets would not put their Clutch City moniker to shame in Game 7. They ended up winning and moving on to the Western Conference finals thanks to 22 points and 13 rebounds from Olajuwon. They were on their way to the Conference finals versus the Utah Jazz.

Despite good outputs from Hakeem, the Rockets lost Games 1 and 2 by double digits before winning Games 3 and 4 on their home court. In both home wins, Olajuwon had 27 points. However, the Jazz took back the series lead by winning Game 5 by five points. Olajuwon did not slack off in that game as he finished with 33 points and 10 rebounds.

Against the Jazz, Olajuwon dominated his competition, overpowering and perplexing the likes of Jazz big men Greg Ostertag, Greg Foster, and Antoine "the Big Dog" Carr, averaging 27.2 points (tops among all players in the series) and 9.3 rebounds per game. However, in the deciding Game 6, despite the Rockets holding a 13-point lead with less than seven minutes remaining in the game, Stockton took control of the game in the final quarter. Stockton poured in 15 point in the fourth quarter, including a series-winning 3-point shot at the buzzer.

## Injury Season, First-Round Exits

Entering the 1997-98 season, it seemed as if Hakeem Olajuwon's body was beginning to fail him. He started the new season slow as he scored 20 or more points only twice in his first 11 games. Though his scoring dipped, Hakeem was still a reliable rebounder and a proficient shot blocker. He had 8 blocks in his second game of the season in a win versus the Sacramento Kings. He also had four double-digit rebounding games in the early part of the season.

Unfortunately for Hakeem, he missed a bunch of games starting from late November of 1997 up to February of 1998. He had been suffering from lingering knee pains in that late part of his career. He underwent arthroscopic surgery on November 24 to fix the issues in his left knee. The Dream went to sleep as he missed as much as two months because of the recovery period following the procedure on his knee.

Hakeem made his return on February 3, 1998. He scored 10 points in 19 minutes as the Rockets won that game against the Grizzlies. He figured in double digits in four of his next five games before going for 21 points and 20 rebounds in a win over the LA Clippers. Though Hakeem Olajuwon maintained his rebounding and defensive prowess as the season was winding down, it seemed that there was something off with his offense. It appeared that Olajuwon's knees could no longer handle the many pivot moves, quick spins, and bursting first steps that were such a big part of his offensive game.

Hakeem finished the regular season averaging what was then a career-low 16.4 points, 9.8 rebounds, 3 assists, 1.8 steals, and 2 blocks in 47 games. His field goal percentage was down to 48% after being above 50% his whole career before the injury. The Rockets suffered a huge blow when they missed them for 35 games. Houston finished with a record of 41-41. They were the eighth seed in the West as they barely made the playoffs. That proves how valuable a player Olajuwon was for the Rockets even at the age of 35.

In the first round, the Rockets pushed the top-seeded Utah Jazz to the limit. They won Game 1 by 13 points as Olajuwon finished with 16 points, 13 rebounds, 5 assists, and 6 blocks. Utah would not lose two games at home as the Rockets lost Game 2 by 15. As the season shifted over to Houston, Hakeem had 28 points and 12 rebounds to lead the Rockets to a 4-point win. However, they would never win a game again as the Jazz took Games 4 and 5. In a 22-point loss in Game 5, the Dream had 27 points, 15 rebounds, and 5 blocks, but made only 10 out of 29 from the field. In the closeout loss, he had 15 points on 7-of-19 shooting.

After the first-round loss to the Utah Jazz, Clyde Drexler decided to hang his sneakers up and retire. Drexler, though way past his prime years, was still capable of putting up about 20 points per night. Nevertheless, he decided that he could no longer handle the grind of another NBA season. Without Drexler, the Houston Rockets' Big Three era was officially over. Nevertheless, they tried to fill Clyde's role by acquiring six-time champion Scottie Pippen in a trade with the Chicago Bulls, who were trying to rebuild as Michael Jordan decided to retire after winning the NBA title for the sixth time in the 1998 playoffs.

Before the start of the new season, the NBA was in a lockout that was a result of a labor dispute between the team owners and the players' union. The dispute was settled in January, and the season only started in February. The regular season was shortened to 50 games and the All-Star Game was canceled. Because of the long offseason break, Hakeem Olajuwon had plenty of time to rest his knees. He came into the 1999 season in a comparatively healthier state than in his 1997-98 version.

The addition of Scottie Pippen much veteran leadership and championship experience to the team. He was also responsible for manning the perimeter defense while Olajuwon handled the paint. The three veterans led the Rockets to a rejuvenated season despite the obvious chemistry issues between Pippen and Barkley. But Hakeem, being the consummate professional, continued to play his heart out.

In 14 games in February, Olajuwon had eight double-double outings. He was also blocking shots left and right as he had at least 1 block in 12 of his first 14 games. He scored in double digits in all but one of those games. In March, he continued playing well, consistently scoring in double digits in all but one game. He had five double-doubles in 17 outings in that month. He even had 31 points and 11 rebounds on March 11 in a win versus the Vancouver Grizzlies. Hakeem then had 32 points and 12 rebounds on March 22 in a win over the Kings.

On the first day of April, Hakeem Olajuwon posted 32 points, 8 rebounds, 4 steals, and 3 blocks in a slim loss to Utah. Nevertheless, he continued to score in double digits in 17 of his next 18 games as the season ended. He had 12 double-double games in that span of games while having at least 1 block in all 18 of those outings. Hakeem had at least 3 blocks in nine of his final 18 games.

Olajuwon averaged 18.9 points, 9.6 rebounds, 1.6 steals, and 2.5 blocks in his 14th year in the NBA. At 36 years old, he was still kicking it against even the younger centers as he was named to the All-NBA Third Team. Olajuwon played all 50 games and averaged nearly 36 minutes per outing. His field goal shooting was up to 51.4% after being down in the high 40s in the previous season. The Houston Rockets won 31 of their 50 games and qualified for the postseason as the fifth seed in the Western Conference.

In the first round of the playoffs, Hakeem rekindled his rivalry with Shaquille O'Neal as the Rockets faced the upstart Los Angeles Lakers. This time, Shaq was the better and healthier pivot man. After scoring 22 points in a loss in Game 1, Hakeem was limited to a total of 13 points and 11 rebounds in his next two outings even as Houston won their lone game in Game 3. In Game 4, he had 18 points and 10 rebounds, but the Lakers won the series in four games. It was then when Olajuwon was finally showing signs of wear and tear as he averaged merely 13.3 points and 7.3 rebounds in the four-game loss to Los Angeles.

## More Injuries, Missing the Playoffs

For a man nearing 37 years of age, Hakeem Olajuwon was still a comparatively good center entering the 1999-2000 season. However, the Rockets were no longer banking on him or even on Barkley. They found a good player in explosive guard Steve Francis, who went on to lead the Rockets in scoring and win the Rookie of the Year award. Cuttino Mobley, off the bench, also added a lot of firepower. The Rockets were looking to rebuild with those two youngsters.

Despite the fact that the Houston Rockets were leaning toward the younger players, Olajuwon still played well to start the 1999-2000 season. He scored in double digits in the first 12 games of the season. On November 18, 1999, he had 31 points in a loss to the Kings. Hakeem had five double-doubles in that span of games. He was even blocking shots at a high rate, as he had at least one block in all but three of his first 12 outings. However, Olajuwon began to slow down. He was diagnosed with blood clots in his leg. The injury caused him to miss more than six weeks.

When Hakeem made his return on January 17, 2000, he came off the bench. His productivity dropped to an all-time low as he struggled to get back to a respectable form for a man of his caliber and accomplishments. His best game after coming back was a 21-point output in a loss to the San Antonio Spurs. As it seemed as if the Rockets would no longer make it to the playoffs, Hakeem Olajuwon was shut down for the remainder of the regular season on March 20.

Hakeem Olajuwon averaged 10.3 points, 6.2 rebounds, 1.6 blocks, and 24 minutes per game. He appeared in 44 games in that season while starting merely 28. The Rockets missed the playoffs with a record of 34-48. It was only the second time that Hakeem missed the postseason in his legendary career as an NBA great.

## Final Season in Houston

When Charles Barkley retired after the 1999-2000 season, Hakeem Olajuwon was the only remainder of Houston's powerhouse team in the 1990s. At 38 years old, he was leading a team full of young talent. At that time, he was no longer the dominant force in the middle he used to be. Hakeem could still play defense at a high level, but his primary role was to serve as the inspiration and the veteran leader for a rebuilding Houston Rockets squad.

Olajuwon started the 2000-01 season scoring double digits in 12 of his first 20 games. He also rebounded in double digits in two of those games. Despite still playing at a particularly good level for a man of his age, Hakeem Olajuwon was still missing games from time to time because of chronic pain in his knee and lingering back injuries.

Although it was a bad season in both production and wins, Hakeem Olajuwon was still able to show the world flashbacks of what he used to be. Most of those games were near the end of the season. In a loss to the Dallas Mavericks on March 3, 2001, Hakeem had 27 points and 13 rebounds. Twenty-two days later, he had 20 points and 11 rebounds in a loss to Phoenix. As the season was nearing its end, he had 26 points and 10 rebounds on April 7 and then 24 points, 9 rebounds, and 6 assists against the Timberwolves in his final game of the season and, unfortunately, for the Houston Rockets.

During the 2000-01 season, Hakeem Olajuwon averaged 11.9 points, 7.4 rebounds, 1.2 steals, 1.5 blocks, and about 27 minutes per game in 58 appearances. The Rockets, with a record of 45 wins to 37 losses, missed the playoffs again. It was the only time Olajuwon missed the postseason in back-to-back years. That season was Hakeem's final one with the Rockets after spending two decades (including college) in Houston.

## Trade to the Raptors, Final NBA Season, Retirement

After the 2000-01 season, Hakeem Olajuwon refused to sign a lucrative extension with the Houston Rockets because he wanted to play elsewhere. He requested to be traded away from the organization where he had spent 16 seasons. When the dust settled, Hakeem was traded to the Toronto Raptors for a few future draft choices. While many people wanted Olajuwon to have retired as a Rocket, it was a bittersweet parting for the man that brought two championships to Houston.

Hakeem joined a Toronto Raptors team that had legitimate playoff aspirations. Toronto had a star player named Vince Carter, who gave them 25 points per night. Aside from Carter, the Raptors also leaned heavily on good role players such as Antonio Davis, Alvin Williams, and Mo Peterson. In that season, Olajuwon came mostly off the bench as a veteran leader for a team that had the makings of a good playoff contender.

As a scorer, Olajuwon was no longer the capable point-maker he had been. He did have several games of scoring in double digits. However, he did most of his damage as a rebounder and as a defender. In the middle of November 2001, Hakeem had three straight double-digit rebounding games. He had back-to-back 12-rebound games before grabbing 20 boards in a loss to Detroit on November 20. As a shot blocker, he had 3 or more blocks in five games of his first 20. He had two games of blocking 7 shots in November. On December 12, he even went up for 9 blocks in a loss to the Spurs. But, as the season went on, lingering back injuries troubled and slowed down the 39-year old Dream.

Olajuwon finished the season averaging career lows of 7.1 points and 6 rebounds to go along with 1.2 steals, and 1.5 blocks. The Toronto Raptors finished with a record of 42-40, which gave them the fifth seed in the Eastern Conference. However, the injury to Vince Carter slowed the team down. They lost to the Detroit Pistons in five games in the first round of the 2002 playoffs. After that series loss, Hakeem Olajuwon officially announced his retirement from basketball.

The Rockets officially retired Olajuwon's number in 2002 and, in 2008, the organization erected a 1,000-pound bronze sculpture outside the team's new Toyota Center. The sculpture features Olajuwon's jersey rather than an image of the man himself in keeping with the tenets of his Muslim faith, which forbids a statue bearing a likeness or picture. Instead of a statue similar to the one the Bulls erected of Jordan in front of the United Center or the one the Lakers did for Magic Johnson outside the Staples Center, Olajuwon's sculpture simply features the legend's career milestones resting on a red granite foundation.

Olajuwon's milestones are certainly worthy of being set in stone. He won a pair of NBA championships (1994, 1995) while being named the NBA Finals MVP each time. In 1994, Olajuwon pulled off the rare feat as he was also named the league's MVP for the 1993-94 season, rewarding him for a season for the ages. Perhaps underscoring how special his 1993-94 season was, Olajuwon also found the 3-point line that season, shooting

.421 percent from behind the arc, connecting on 8 of his 19 attempts.

He earned All-NBA First Team honors six times in his 18-year career (1987-89, 1993-94, and 1997). Olajuwon was also named to the All-NBA Second Team three times (1986, 1990, and 1996) and he received Third Team honors three times as well (1991, 1995, and 1999). While Olajuwon's offense, highlighted by his many low-post scoring moves, often gained the most media attention, he was also a two-time NBA Defensive Player of Year (1993, 1994), a five-time All-Defensive First Team (1987, 1988, 1990, 1993, 1994) and a four-time All-Defensive Second Team (1985, 1991, 1996, 1997).

His overall game garnered an even dozen All-Star selections and a gold medal with the 1996 Olympic Team in Atlanta. In 1996, he was named one of the 50 greatest players in NBA history. Olajuwon ended his career in the top 10 all-time in blocks, scoring, rebounding, and steals. He is the only player in NBA history to retire in the top 10 for all four categories. Olajuwon was elected to the Basketball Hall of Fame in 2008.

# Chapter 5: Olajuwon's Personal Life

A cornerstone of Olajuwon's life has always been his Islamic faith. He is a devout Muslim who was known to carry a compass so he knew which direction Mecca stood from whichever NBA arena he happened to be playing on any particular night. Though he was raised in the Muslim faith, it was not until early in his NBA career that Olajuwon reconnected with Islam. Olajuwon's beliefs are credited with helping him to maintain his focus on the court and live a clean lifestyle off the court. His faith would often test his resolve during the holy month of Ramadan. During the month, Muslims abstain from food or water during daylight hours, fasting from sunrise to sunset – not an easy task when the NBA schedule called for a daytime game or at a minimum practice sessions.

Rather than depleting his talents, Olajuwon channeled the willpower needed to stay away from the basic temptation of reaching for some water during a game by often raising the level of his play to new heights. In February 1995, Ramadan started on the first of the month. Yet Olajuwon continued to play and he won NBA Player of the Month honors.

While some fans and perhaps teammates may have wished that their big man would had stayed hydrated during a day game, Olajuwon would remain true to his faith and continue the same routine he would be practicing if he was not in the NBA: Awakening before sunrise to eat seven dates and drink a gallon of water. A prayer for strength would follow, after which Olajuwon would abstain from food or liquid until sunset.

Olajuwon continues to follow his faith devoutly, spending a good portion of his time in the Middle East, pursuing Islamic studies in Amman, Jordan. Olajuwon married his current wife, Dalia Asafi, in 1996 and the couple has two daughters together. Olajuwon also has one daughter with his former wife Lita Spencer, whom he met in college. His eldest daughter, Abisola, has followed in her father's footsteps, having played professionally in the WNBA and in Europe. Nowadays, Olajuwon keeps busy by investing in real estate and serving as Chairman and CEO of the DR34M mansion and as the founder of the Dream

Foundation for Humanitarian Aid in Africa, Jordan, and Houston.

Olajuwon also has a strong appreciation for fashion and he has started his own clothing line. He was inspired in part by the difficulty for someone his size to find clothing, even a major metropolitan area such as Houston. The search for clothing that fit a 7-foot man pushed Olajuwon to open a high-end menswear and luxury leather clothing goods and accessories store (DR34M) occupying a 17,000-square-foot historic mansion in suburban Houston.

However, Olajuwon understands that the world needs more than high-end clothing. Due in part to his modest upbringing, Olajuwon endorsed Spalding basketball shoes because they were cheaper and more affordable than Nike, Reebok and Adidas. Recently, Olajuwon has entered a business deal with athletic performance footwear and clothing company Etonic to launch Brand Dream, where Olajuwon will collaborate with marketing and development groups at Etonic to create footwear, apparel and a line of accessories. The deal will also bring to market a limited issue re-issue of Olajuwon's 1984 Akeem the

Dream signature shoes (Olajuwon wore Etonic shoes as a rookie before signing a deal with L.A. Gear and before signing his long-term deal with Spalding).

# Chapter 6: Impact on Basketball

Olajuwon was inducted into the Naismith Memorial Basketball Hall of Fame as part of its 2008 class of inductees. Joining Olajuwon in that year's class were television announcer and former coach Dick Vitale, who gave Olajuwon the "Dream" nickname when he was a freshman at the University of Houston. It was more than a dream career for Olajuwon, who completed his 18-year NBA career with 27,000 points, 13,747 rebounds, and 3,830 blocks.

Also sharing the stage with Olajuwon was fellow inductee and long-time competitor Patrick Ewing. The two big men have shared many similar moments throughout their athletic careers, as the pair faced off in both the NCAA Championship Game (advantage Ewing) and the NBA finals (advantage Olajuwon). The duo also shares a somewhat similar upbringing. Like Olajuwon, Ewing was born outside the United States. Ewing was 12 years old when he moved from Jamaica to America. Like Olajuwon, Ewing also felt like he found his identity playing basketball in the U.S. Also like Olajuwon, Ewing's career marks also bear some similarities has Ewing also played in three NCAA Final Fours, scored just under 25,000 points and grabbed 11,607 rebounds in his NBA career. Ewing was also an Olympic gold medalist (twice) and, while Olajuwon retired with a bevy of all-time Rockets records, Ewing left his mark on New York as the Knicks' career leader in points, rebounds, blocked shots, and steals. Olajuwon credited Ewing with providing him with a benchmark regarding his own play throughout his career, citing the need to be the best one has to play against the best.

Olajuwon also took time to thank those who mentored him through the years, especially his coaches. He credited his college coach at the University of Houston Guy Lewis, who provided motivation through demanding the best, and helping Olajuwon to understand that sometimes your best is not good enough because he knew that his young center could perform even better. Olajuwon went on to praise Bill Fitch of the Rockets, his first coach as a professional. Fitch was able to take pressure off of Olajuwon being the top overall draft pick by putting more pressure on him. He also praised his final coach with the Rockets, Rudy Tomjanovich, for allowing Olajuwon to grow into the leadership role and responsibility that Tomjanovich entrusted to him. Olajuwon also had special praise for Moses Malone, who helped him mature as a young player as Malone helped transform Olajuwon from a bench-sitting prospect into a college basketball force to be reckoned with.

There is no doubt that Olajuwon has had mentors along the way on his transition from a young handball-playing boy in Nigeria to being enshrined in the Basketball Hall of Fame. More than 30 African players have stepped on an NBA court since Olajuwon began his professional career. No doubt, these players had Olajuwon as a role model in making the transition from Africa to the NBA with hard work and class, in the way he conducted himself off the court, and in how hard he worked to improve his game.

One such player about to make his mark on the NBA is Kansas Jayhawk's 7-foot center Joel Embiid, who is from the African nation of Cameroon. Though today's one-and-done scenario makes it hard to compare the two players statistically, they are similar in their sizes, nationalities

(Cameroon and Nigeria border one another), the relatively late age that both began to play basketball, and the pre-draft media attention (Embiid is predicted to be a top-three pick in the 2014 NBA Draft). But statistics do tell a few stories of similarity. Olajuwon was a terrific rebounder who worked hard to block out his opponents and keep them away from the boards while possessing a great sense of where missed shots were heading after coming off the rim or backboard. Olajuwon averaged 13.5 rebounds per game per 40 minutes of play as a freshman, while Embiid, who seems to possess many of the same rebounding traits as Olajuwon as a freshman, averaged 13.3 rebounds per game.

During Embiid's early days playing organized basketball in Cameroon, his coaches gave him videotape of Olajuwon and told him to watch it every day. So Embiid watched the tape after every practice, studying Olajuwon's game, his footwork, and his remarkable agility for such a big man. The video study not only helped to define Embiid's own game, but it provided him with the mental edge he needed to make the move from Africa to the United States and follow in Olajuwon's footsteps. University of Kansas head coach Bill Self noticed the similarities between Embiid and Olajuwon, stating that while Embiid is his own player, the incredible footwork and agility for such a raw basketball player reminds him of a young Olajuwon in his early days at the University of Houston.

While Olajuwon's success at the University of Houston brought national attention to the previously unknown Nigerian handball player, the many milestones he reached along the way on his Hall of Fame career helped to keep Phi Slama Jama in the minds of college basketball fans ever since. Today, the NCAA tournament is one of the biggest annual events on the American sporting calendar. Tournament semifinal and Final Four games are usually played in domed football stadiums designed to hold tens of thousands of fans. While the NCAA tournament was definitely popular at the time of Olajuwon's college career, the entertaining style of play that Phi Slama Jama featured appealed to a broad audience and helped capture the attention of casual fans and brought them closer to the sport. The continued success of Olajuwon and Drexler helped to perpetuate the importance of those Houston Cougars squads, even in defeat. The Phi Slama Jama aura added even more drama to the improbable North Carolina State NCAA championship, now featured throughout the sports media world through avenues such as ESPN's 30-for-30 documentary series. The TV broadcasts of Phi Slama Jama games, such as the 1983 Final between Houston and North Carolina State (18.6 million households) and the preceding Houston-Louisville national semifinal (14.8 million) were ratings records at the time and set the wheels in motion for the multiple media channels and outlets – both digital and print – that cover college basketball games today.

Though now famous from his successes in both college and the NBA, Olajuwon has never sought out the limelight or frolicked in his own fame. Rather, he has always been one to give back to others instead of seeking out attention to feed his ego. That does not keep others from bestowing honors upon Olajuwon, of course: He recently accepted the title of NBA ambassador to Africa. Olajuwon plans on working closely with the NBA Africa office in

Johannesburg, South Africa, and assisting on projects such as player development and NBA Cares charitable events. Olajuwon also hopes to bring messages of hope and positivity to help alleviate crises on the continent, such as the current troubles in Nigeria. Far from a lofty title, Olajuwon expects to be on the ground in Africa whenever possible and when his impact is most needed.

Olajuwon has returned to Africa throughout the years, lending his name, assistance and financial contributions to aid the people of his former continent. He recently participated in the launch of "Power Forward," an NBA-sponsored development program launched in the Nigerian capital city of Abuja last November. The program included the dedication of a basketball court and a coaching clinic for more than 300 students from 10 secondary schools throughout Abuja. Before that, he visited South Africa in August 2013 and attended the Nelson Mandela Sport and Culture Day celebrations at the International Convention Centre and the FNB Stadium in Johannesburg. Olajuwon is sometimes joined on his charitable visits to Africa by fellow African-born players, such as Oklahoma City's

Serge Ibaka, former NBA great Dikembe Mutombo, or those making their first trip, such as WNBA star Swin Cash.

Olajuwon gives credit to his religious faith with helping him to remain grounded despite his wealth and global fame. Olajuwon, who openly talks about living by principles such as honesty, kindness, and community service, remains true to his words. In addition to his work with existing charitable organizations such as UNICEF and the Make-A-Wish Foundation, Olajuwon also founded the Dream Foundation, which awards college scholarships to high school students. Because of values instilled in him by his parents at an early age, Olajuwon, who reportedly speaks five languages, treasures education and the opportunities it affords to those who seek it out.

# Chapter 7: Olajuwon's Legacy and Future

While the role of the big man has changed since Olajuwon's playing days and the number of true centers making contributions on NBA rosters has lessened over the years, he is still revered as a living icon by those who man the middle. Olajuwon has been known to work with today's centers (and center/power forward hybrid players) and he conducts low-post move sessions from his ranch in suburban Houston, though he has also made house calls, as he did in 2012. Olajuwon had worked with Amar'e Stoudemire of the New York Knicks in Texas. The teaching went so well that then head coach Mike Woodson invited Olajuwon to take his show on the road to the Big Apple and work out some more with Stoudemire, as well as Carmelo Anthony, Tyson Chandler, Marcus Camby and the team's other big men.

Centers in today's NBA certainly benefit from the past play of big men such as Olajuwon, who helped form the center position from a primarily defensive role to a position on the court that can carry a team's offensive load. In some ways, Olajuwon was a precursor to some of today's centers like Tim Duncan, who has his own shake-and-bake type of moves designed to gain enough separation from a defender to get off his shot.

In other ways, the lineage from players such as Olajuwon and even David Robinson of the San Antonio Spurs is disappearing. During Olajuwon's playing days, most successful teams in the league had a big man down low – whether it was a center, such as Olajuwon, Robinson, Abdul-Jabbar or Ewing, or a power forward, such as Charles Barkley, Karl Malone or Shawn Kemp. Today's NBA is much more guard- and shooter-oriented, likely resulting – at least in part – from hand-checking rules and other handcuffs on defensive play that were not a part of the game during Olajuwon's days.

One thing that Olajuwon did for NBA players was to provide a road map for a clean-living and long-lasting career in the league. Not that there is anything wrong with having a corporate mindset and wanting to make as much money off the court as possible, but Olajuwon kept his sponsorships to a minimum. And not that religion or holding beliefs is a prerequisite for living a clean life, but Olajuwon was rarely mentioned in a negative light during his NBA career, either on the court (he always maintained a reputation as a good sportsman) or out in the community.

Olajuwon came to basketball prominence from relative obscurity in a time when international scouting was not a high priority in either college basketball or the professional ranks. The success of Olajuwon foreshadowed the prominence of international-born players in the future of basketball. For example, the San Antonio Spurs have been the NBA's model franchise over the past decade while featuring stars born outside the 50 states in Tim Duncan (U.S. Virgin Islands), Manu Ginobili (Argentina) and Tony Parker (France). Dallas' Dirk Nowitzki (Germany) and Los Angeles Laker Pau Gasol (Spain) have also made their mark in the league and won NBA championships.

# Final Word/About the Author

I was born and raised in Norwalk, Connecticut. Growing up, I could often be found spending many nights watching basketball, soccer, and football matches with my father in the family living room. I love sports and everything that sports can embody. I believe that sports are one of most genuine forms of competition, heart, and determination. I write my works to learn more about influential athletes in the hopes that from my writing, you the reader can walk away inspired to put in an equal if not greater amount of hard work and perseverance to pursue your goals. If you enjoyed *Hakeem Olajuwon: The Remarkable Story of One of 90s Basketball's Greatest Centers,* please leave a review! Also, you can read more of my works on *Colin Kaepernick, Aaron Rodgers, Peyton Manning, Tom Brady, Russell Wilson, Michael Jordan, LeBron James, Kyrie Irving, Klay Thompson, Stephen Curry, Kevin Durant, Russell Westbrook, Anthony Davis, Chris Paul, Blake Griffin, Kobe Bryant, Joakim Noah, Scottie Pippen, Carmelo Anthony, Kevin Love, Grant Hill, Tracy McGrady, Vince Carter, Patrick Ewing, Karl Malone,*

*Tony Parker, Allen Iverson, Reggie Miller, Michael Carter-Williams, John Wall, James Harden, Tim Duncan, Steve Nash, Pau Gasol, Marc Gasol, Jimmy Butler, Dirk Nowitzki, Draymond Green, Pete Maravich, Kawhi Leonard, Dwyane Wade, Ray Allen and Paul George* in the Kindle Store. If you love basketball, check out my website at [claytongeoffreys.com](claytongeoffreys.com) to join my exclusive list where I let you know about my latest books and give you lots of goodies.

# Like what you read? Please leave a review!

I write because I love sharing the stories of influential people like Hakeem Olajuwon with fantastic readers like you. My readers inspire me to write more so please do not hesitate to let me know what you thought by leaving a review! If you love books on life, basketball, or productivity, check out my website at claytongeoffreys.com to join my exclusive list where I let you know about my latest books. Aside from being the first to hear about my latest releases, you can also download a free copy of *33 Life Lessons: Success Principles, Career Advice & Habits of Successful People*. See you there!

*Clayton*

Made in United States
North Haven, CT
13 July 2023

39011678R00065